UNIVERSITY CLASSICS *for*
HIGH SCHOOLS — COLLEGES — UNIVERSITIES

IDYLLS OF THE KING

IDYLLS OF THE KING

BY

ALFRED TENNYSON

EDITED WITH INTRODUCTION, EXPLANATORY
NOTES, AND QUESTIONS FOR CLASS STUDY

BY

HARRIET E. TOWNE
DIRECTOR OF THE CHILD WELFARE BUREAU, PUBLIC SCHOOLS,
LINCOLN, NEBRASKA; FORMERLY TEACHER OF ENGLISH
IN THE LINCOLN HIGH SCHOOL

AND

J. W. SEARSON
FORMERLY PROFESSOR OF ENGLISH, UNIVERSITY OF NEBRASKA,
LINCOLN

Lincoln   Chicago   Dallas   New York
THE UNIVERSITY PUBLISHING COMPANY

The University Classics Series

Uniform With This Volume

Idylls of the King

The Merchant of Venice

Macbeth

The Lady of the Lake

Silas Marner

Julius Cæsar

Selected Poems of Wordsworth

Poe's Poems and Tales

A Midsummer Night's Dream

Hamlet

Selected Poems of Browning

A Tale of Two Cities

Ivanhoe

Milton's Minor Poems

As You Like It

Treasure Island

Other Volumes in Preparation

CONTENTS

INTRODUCTION

How Tennyson Came to Write the Idylls

The story of King Arthur possessed a peculiar fascination for the poet Tennyson. He saw in the story, rightly told, a charming human-interest explanation of life. He thereupon resolved to tell the Arthurian story in a cycle of poems in which his finest art should have expression. For more than fifty years he worked to put these poems in their final shape, now known as "Idylls of the King."

Before studying the Idylls, it is well to know something of the life of Alfred Tennyson, for his life and poems are inseparably connected. He was born August 6, 1809, the birth-year of Gladstone, Darwin, and Lincoln. His childhood was spent in a cultured country home in Somersby amid the most beautiful outdoor scenes in rural England. He loved the country with its gardens, farms, brooks, birds, and flowers, but most of all he loved the sea whose rhythmic pulse-beats found their way into his poetry. While in Trinity College, Cambridge, he began his serious life work as a poet, and from 1830 until his death in 1892, his finest energies were devoted to an artistic interpretation of the best in the life around him. With the death of his dearest friend, Arthur Henry Hallam, the young poet left the dream world of youth and entered the real world of joy and sorrow where faith in God and the belief in immortality of the soul seemed indispensable. It is not surprising, therefore, that Tennyson should desire to crown his career with the broadest and richest interpretation of human life struggling toward the ideal.

In his earliest poems, such as *Mariana, The Miller's Daughter, The Palace of Art,* and *A Dream of Fair Women,* he had shown a wonderful perfection of form and sense of beauty. In such poems as *Locksley Hall, Lady Clara Vere de Vere, The May Queen, Ulysses, Dora,* and *Morte d'Arthur,* he had combined beauty of form with power to interpret truth close to the heart. Then came *The Princess, In Memoriam,* and other poems adding to the lustre of his name.

But most of all his heart was set on creating a series of Idylls, or pictures, each to treat of one important phase in the story of the great King Arthur. Twelve of these *pictures* he created, and together they form "*Idylls of the King.*" The whole poem is a parable, a story of living men and women, told charmingly as "the dream of man coming into practical life and ruined by one sin," as Tennyson himself declared. Then he added: "It is not the history of one man or of one generation, but of a whole cycle of generations," a tale

"New-old, and shadowing Sense at war with Soul."

Here are the names of the twelve Idylls, five of which may serve as types of all for the purpose of closer study and appreciation:

    I. The Coming of Arthur
   II. Gareth and Lynette (gâr′ĕth, lī-nĕt′)

TENNYSON'S POETRY

To summarize briefly the leading characteristics of Tennyson's poetry, we may well quote, in part, the estimate given by Dr. Henry van Dyke, personal friend of Tennyson, and America's most authoritative editor and interpreter of Tennyson's works. Doctor van Dyke gives us the following six striking characteristics of Tennyson's poetry:

1. "His diction is singularly lucid, smooth, and melodious. He has the power of expressing the vague, delicate, yet potent emotions, the feelings that belong to the twilight of the heart, when the glow of love and the shadow of regret are mingled, in melodies of words as simple and as magical as the chime of far-off bells, or the echoes of a bugle-call crying among the hills. . . .

2. "He has an extraordinary truthfulness and delicacy of touch in natural description. . . .

3. "His range of imaginative sympathy, as shown in

his ballads and character pieces, is very wide; but it moves for the most part along natural and normal rather than strange and eccentric lines.

4. "His work reflects with singular fidelity the scientific and social movements of the age. . . .

5. "As in its form, so in its spirit, the verse of Tennyson expresses a constant and controlling sense of law and order. . . .

6. "The poetry of Tennyson is pervaded by a profoundly religious spirit."—From *Library of the World's Best Literature*, Article on *Tennyson*.

Idylls of the King is a poem which finely reveals these qualities. In the use of rhythmical tones and perfect meters, in the exquisite choice of words and phrasing, and in skill to fit words to subtle meanings with indefinable charm, Tennyson has shown himself a perfect master. In each of the *Idylls*, added pleasure comes from observing the clear smooth diction, the magical phrasing, the detailed accuracy of his cameo-like descriptions, all blended in the charm of musical words set to perfect meter.

Suggested Study Helps

The literature of the Arthurian story is extensive, and only a very little of it can be consulted here. Sidney Lanier's edition of *Malory's Boys' King Arthur* is helpful and interesting. Edward Brooks's *Story of King Arthur and His Knights of the Round Table* may be read with profit. Bulfinch's *Age of Chivalry*, Church's *Heroes of Chivalry and Romance*, Hamilton Wright

Mabie's *Heroes Every Child Should Know* (Chapters on
Arthur and Sir Galahad), and the article on *The
Arthurian Legend* in Warner's *Library of the World's
Best Literature*, will be of great help in the study. Henry
van Dyke's *The Poetry of Tennyson*, Stopford Brooke's
Tennyson—His Art and Relation to Modern Life,
Richard Jones's *The Growth of the Idylls of the King*,
and Harold Littledale's *Essays on Tennyson's Idylls of
the King* contain interesting commentaries and esti-
mates. G. F. Watts's *Sir Galahad* and the famous
Abbey series of Holy Grail paintings in the Boston
Public Library are among the finest of the artistic
interpretations of the great legend.

SOURCES OF THE STORY OF
KING ARTHUR

King Arthur was the romantic leader of the Christian Britons in their struggles against the heathen Saxon
invaders in the sixth century. First, in twelve fiercely-
fought battles, the Christians overcame the heathen,
but later Britain was overrun by the Saxon hosts. In
the twelfth century, Geoffrey of Monmouth wrote in
Latin his *History of the Kings of Britain*, containing the
outline of the tale of Britain's great King Arthur. Then
followed Layamon's *Brut*, Chrestien de Troyes' *Lancelot*, Wolfram von Eschenbach's *Parzival and the Holy
Grail*, during the later twelfth and thirteenth centuries,
while the crusading spirit was at its height and "knighthood was in flower." Finally, about 1470, Sir Thomas
Malory wove these tales happily into his own complete

story of Britain's hero in *Le Morte d'Arthur*. Early in Tennyson's career as a poet, the Lady Charlotte Guests' translation of Old Welsh legends, *The Mabinogion*, appeared and added fuel to the young poet's flame of enthusiasm for the heroic tales of his country's early history. From these and other sources Tennyson drew freely, then retold the stories in his own charming manner to interpret their larger meaning in the great story of human living.

SUMMARY OF IDYLLS OF THE KING

The twelve pictures or idylls set forth the reign of King Arthur "from his supernatural coming, through his conquest and beneficent reign, to his fall and departure." Underneath the charming story is a deep allegorical meaning. As van Dyke says, the whole plan "is a parable of the life of man." King Arthur represents the soul struggling against the flesh or the temptations of the world. These temptations appear in the form of his enemies and later in the form of the worldliness and corruption of his knights. Arthur is presented as the ideal knight and king in contrast with the more human type such as Lancelot, Gawain, Modred, and others.

To summarize the completed poem, *The Coming of Arthur* tells of Arthur's mysterious origin, his conquest of Britain with the assistance of Merlin, his winning of Guinevere, and his twelve great victories over the Saxons. *Gareth and Lynette* is an attractive tale of a youthful knight's winning a lady through deep humility toward her and through great valor displayed against gigantic foes. *The Marriage of Geraint* and *Geraint and Enid* tell a romantic tale of a brave young knight who rescued and wedded a beautiful young girl, and of her heroism and devotion when her husband tried her by an undeserved test. *Balin and Balan* shows the evil effects of the poison of jealousy and guilty love. The rumor of Guinevere's guilt spread rapidly by the aid of the jealous Vivien, mistress of Mark of Cornwall, Arthur's rival. This wicked rumor at once maddens Balin the savage, a worshipper of the Queen. He immediately offers insult to her colors and fights with his brother Balan a duel in which both are slain. *Merlin and Vivien* continues the story of Vivien who now comes to Arthur's court, spreads the foulest scandals, and finally captivates by her flatteries, Merlin, the old magician. Having been taught by him a secret charm, she uses it to imprison the magician in the hollow of an old oak.

Lancelot and Elaine tells of the relations between Guinevere and Lancelot whose guilty loves are being whispered far and wide throughout the realm. Lancelot spurns the pure maiden love of Elaine, lily maid of Astolat, and continues 'falsely true' to Queen Guinevere. In *The Holy Grail*, King Arthur's knights ride out to seek the vision of the Grail. Three of them, Galahad, Percival, and Bors, because of their fine spiritual gifts, see the vision and retire from the world to a life of holy meditation. Others soon abandon the quest and many of them perish. Because of his guilty love for Guinevere, Lancelot is denied a vision of the Grail.

The gradual loosening of the ties that bound the round table is set forth in *Pelleas and Etarre* and the *Last Tournament*. All but the King know of the guilty love of Lancelot and Guinevere. Etarre unblushingly spurns the devotion of Pelleas for that of Gawain. Tristram openly proclaims his infidelity to Isolt, wife of Mark of Cornwall, and scoffs at all bonds of loyalty and affection. In *Guinevere*, Modred and Vivien report to King Arthur the guilty love of Lancelot and the Queen. Lancelot at once departs for his kingdom overseas and Guinevere retires to a convent. On his way to fight with the rebellious Modred, Arthur stops at the convent, rebukes the Queen, forgives her, and bids her farewell.

The Passing of Arthur tells of the last battle of the King when he was mortally wounded by Modred and of his mysterious departure to the supernatural world from which he is to come again to rule over his people.

It is well to give a somewhat fuller summary of the five Idylls to be studied and appreciated in detail. A mere glance at each of the following more detailed summaries will give but a slight hint of the riches that await one who reads these stories with fine appreciation.

THE COMING OF ARTHUR

Leodogran, King of Cameliard, had an only daughter, Guinevere, "fairest of all flesh on earth." In order to save and strengthen his tottering kingdom, he appealed for help to Arthur, newly crowned king of Britain. At the head of his knights, Arthur drove out the heathen and restored law and order. Meanwhile, Arthur longed to have the beautiful Guinevere as his queen, for he had "felt the light of her eyes into his life smite on the sudden" as first he rode against the heathen. But new difficulties arose. The lords and barons of the realm conspired with "a score of petty kings" to overthrow him, for they declared that he was not fit to rule, for he was not even of royal birth. In giant battle, he overthrew the hosts of the conspirators and immediately sent messengers to Leodogran asking Guinevere's hand as the price of his service. Unwilling to give his daughter in marriage to one of less than royal birth, Leodogran inquires carefully into the circumstances attending the "coming" of Arthur. What follows, satisfies Leodogran that Arthur is worthy, and Arthur and Guinevere are solemnly united at Camelot. Resisted by Roman authority, King Arthur, consolidated the petty princedoms and "in twelve great battles overcame the heathen hordes, and made a realm and reigned."

GARETH AND LYNETTE

Gareth, younger brother of Gawain and Modred, who have already become knights at the court of King Arthur, wishes to follow his brothers and win his spurs as a true knight. His mother, Bellicent, half sister of Arthur, is reluctant to have him go. Finally she consents to his going on condition that he will conceal his name and serve at court as a mere kitchen attendant for a whole year. With two servants he slips away to Camelot where he is met by Merlin, who soon discovers his secret. He is permitted to enter the great hall of King Arthur where the King is sending one knight after another to restore the wrongs reported to him. Gareth asks that the King make him a kitchen servant for a year, after which he will reveal his name and ask to be sent on a quest to prove his right to knighthood. For a month, he serves under the court steward, Kay, who dislikes and mistreats him. Then his mother repents of her severity, sends him knightly arms, and frees him from his vow of kitchen service. Gareth goes to the King, reveals his name, is secretly made a knight, and is sent to release the Lady Lyonors, sister of Lynette, from the Castle Perilous where she is imprisoned by four wicked knights, Sir Morning-Star, Sir Noon-Sun, Sir Evening-Star, and Sir Death. Lynette, appearing at court, has asked that the great knight Lancelot be sent on this perilous quest. Instead, the King has given her the young knight Gareth and she runs from the hall in disgust at having a mere kitchen slave as a champion. Gareth, closely followed by Lancelot, overtakes Lynette and offers her safe escort, which she refuses insolently. Sir Kay overtook Gareth, attacked him, and was overthrown while Lynette still mocked him as a kitchen servant. When at last they come to the river surrounding the Castle Perilous, Gareth in turn overthrows Sir Morning-Star, Sir Noon-Sun, and Sir Evening-Star. Now Lynette relents, asks Gareth's pardon, and requests him to ride at her side. They stop for rest and food in a hermit's cave on whose rough walls is a huge carving representing the war of Time against the Human Soul.

Meanwhile, Lancelot overtakes them and mistakingly fights with Gareth and easily overthrows him. Lynette's disgust for Gareth returns until she finds that the victor is none other than Lancelot himself and that her comrade Gareth is a royal prince. The next morning Gareth rides forth fearlessly and attacks the last foe, Sir Death, whose helmet is split at a single blow only to reveal the rosy face of a little lad who had been dressed in this horrible disguise by his brothers, who felt that even the stoutest heart would shrink from fighting Sir Death. Gareth enters the castle, wins his quest, and also the fair Lady Lynette.

The story clearly reveals the discipline of ambition through obedience and "the victories of true nobility over false pride."

LANCELOT AND ELAINE

As the story opens, Elaine, lily maid of Astolat, sits in her tower guarding the shield of an unknown knight. In eight successive tournaments, the great knight Lancelot had won the eight successive diamond prizes offered by King Arthur. He was keeping them until he should win the ninth when he would give them all to Arthur's queen, Guinevere. On pretence of illness, Guinevere remains away from the ninth tournament and Lancelot, on pretext of a wound, remains with her. The Queen challenges him to go to the tournament in disguise and win the ninth diamond as an unknown knight.

On his way to the tournament, he stops at Astolat where he is received as a noble guest and where he borrows the shield of Sir Torre, the oldest son. The lord of the castle arranges to send with him to the tournament his younger son, Sir Lavaine, as his companion. Meanwhile Elaine, simple, sweet, and lovable, falls in love with Lancelot, who has been so courteous to her; and she gives him a red sleeve, embroidered with pearls, which she begs him to wear as her favor in the lists. Although he has never before worn the favor of any lady, he consents to wear this thinking that it will complete his disguise. He then intrusts to her his own shield and rides away with Lavaine.

At the tournament, Lancelot enters on the weaker side where his own kindred combine against him because of his complete disguise. Although sorely wounded, he wins the contest and Lavaine carries him half dead to the cave of a friendly hermit. The King sends Sir Gawain with the diamond to find the unknown knight and to deliver to him the prize. When the Queen hears from the King that Lancelot wore a lady's favor on his helmet, she burns with secret jealousy for she is certain that Lancelot has played her false. Meanwhile, Gawain rides aimlessly in search of the stranger knight. Finally he comes to Astolat where he makes love to Elaine, but Elaine shows him the shield she is keeping and confesses that Lancelot, whose shield is immediately recognized by Gawain, is the only man she can ever love. Gawain then intrusts her with the diamond and instructs her to deliver the diamond to Lancelot, and rides away. Then Elaine seeks Lancelot in the lonely hermit's cave and nurses him back to life and together they return to Astolat. On his departure, as Lancelot is about to leave the castle, he asks Elaine, to whom he owes his life, to name the thing she wishes for most. Her answer is "your love." Lancelot tells her that he will never marry but offers her half his lands across the sea as a reward. Then Lancelot, at the request of her father, who thought to break her love, rides away without even so much as looking back at Elaine or waving her a farewell.

Meanwhile, Elaine pines away. Her body is placed in state upon a barge, and the dumb servant of the house rows her slowly up the river to Camelot. When the funeral barge arrives at the castle, King Arthur opens the letter which the maid had written, and which the father and brothers at her request had placed in her lily hand. It tells of her unreturned love for Lancelot and asks him to pray for her soul. Lancelot is struck with the strange contrast between the pure tender love of Elaine and the fierce, jealous passion of Guinevere, and he resolves to be no longer false to his king, King Arthur of the Round Table.

THE HOLY GRAIL

After an adventurous career as a knight, Sir Percivale, called by King Arthur, the Pure, retired to a monastery to lead "the silent life of prayer." The story of this Idyll is developed in the dialogue between Percivale as narrator and the simple-minded Ambrosius as questioner. Percivale tells of the Holy Grail, of how his pious sister, a nun, saw it in a holy vision, and of how she inspired him to go on the quest. Likewise the beautiful young Galahad was inspired by the nun's vision, and, as he sat in Merlin's chair, the seat perilous, the Holy Grail appeared concealed in a luminous cloud. Many knights took the vow to seek the Grail, among them Percivale, Galahad, Sir Bors, Lancelot, and Gawain.

Meanwhile, King Arthur returned from a successful campaign, learned of the vows taken, and, although he frowned upon the enterprise as disastrous to his Order, insisted that the vows be performed. After a glorious tournament, the knights depart. Percivale tells of the phantom-like and real experiences through which he passed, and of his joining Galahad in the final quest where the Holy Vision appeared and Galahad was transported to realms spiritual. Then follow the tales of the successful quest of Sir Bors and of Lancelot's somewhat doubtful triumph. Sir Gawain confessed frankly that he had given up the quest for merest pleasure.

King Arthur reminds his knights of his dark forebodings from the first, for, as predicted, of all those knights who set forth on the quest, "scarce returned a tithe." He reminds them that the king's duty is to guard and rule the land and, in the human way, follow his highest visions. On the whole, this Idyll contains the essence of the spiritual philosophy of Tennyson and of the entire group of *Idylls of the King*.

THE PASSING OF ARTHUR

The story opens with a great battle in which the rebellious forces, under the traitor Modred, fight against King Arthur and his knights. The opposing armies, engaged in the dark confusion of a heavy mist, destroy each other. King Arthur, mortally wounded, strikes down the traitor Modred. Sir Bedivere, last of the faithful knights of the round table, attends the stricken King, who now commands him to throw his sword, Excalibur, into the lake, where long since he had received it from the hand of the Lady of the Lake. When Bedivere ponders on the beauty of the richly jewelled hilt, his love of treasure overcomes his sense of loyalty to the King, so he hides the sword in the reeds at the edge of the lake and makes an incomplete report to the King. A second time Sir Bedivere returned to the lake and was again overcome by selfish desire. A third time the King sent him on a mission, and this time he performed it faithfully, watching the mysterious hand of the Lady of the Lake take back into the deep the great sword Excalibur. Then he placed the dying King on the black barge which bore him mysteriously into the dark of the lake mists whence, years before, he had issued forth in a cloud of mystery.

The central thought of this entire poem is that of the relentless struggle between Sense and Soul. It is represented first in the fierce battles culminating in the conflict between Modred and Arthur. It is represented again in the struggle within the mind of Bedivere to carry out the command of the King. The old order had passed away yielding place to new, and the earth was still left peopled by those who should do God's will in fulfilling the truth uttered by the dying King:

> "The whole round earth is every way
> Bound by gold chains about the feet of God."

Idylls of the King

THE COMING OF ARTHUR

Leodogran, the King of Cameliard,[1]
Had one fair daughter, and none other child;
And she was fairest of all flesh on earth,
Guinevere,[2] and in her his one delight.

For many a petty king ere Arthur[3] came
Ruled in this isle, and ever waging war
Each upon other, wasted all the land;
And still from time to time the heathen host[4]
Swarm'd overseas, and harried[5] what was left.
And so there grew great tracts of wilderness,   10
Wherein the beast was ever more and more,
But man was less and less, till Arthur came.
For first Aurelius[6] lived and fought and died,
And after him King Uther[7] fought and died,
But either fail'd to make the kingdom one.   15

[1] Leodogran (lē ŏd' ō grăn) is one of the petty kings referred to in
line 5. Cameliard (Căm' ĕl árd) is of uncertain location, probably in
what is now Scotland.

[2] Pronounced gwĭn' ĕ vēr.

[3] A Celtic chieftain of Britain in the sixth century, the hero of
Malory's *Le Morte d'Arthur*.

[4] German tribes—Jutes, Angles, Saxons.

[5] Plundered, robbed.

[6] Emperor of Britain, Gaul, and Spain, brother of Uther who followed him on the throne. See *Gareth and Lynette*, note 57.

[7] Predecessor and reputed father of King Arthur.

1

And after these King Arthur for a space,
And thro' the puissance[8] of his Table Round,[9]
Drew all their petty princedoms under him,
Their king and head, and made a realm, and reign'd.

20   And thus the land of Cameliard was waste,
Thick with wet woods, and many a beast therein,
And none or few to scare or chase the beast;
So that wild dog, and wolf and boar and bear
Came night and day, and rooted in the fields,
25 And wallow'd in the gardens of the King.
And ever and anon the wolf would steal
The children and devour, but now and then,
Her own brood lost or dead, lent her fierce teat
To human sucklings; and the children, housed
30 In her foul den, there at their meat would growl,
And mock their foster-mother on four feet,
Till, straighten'd, they grew up to wolflike men,[10]
Worse than the wolves. And King Leodogran
Groan'd for the Roman legions here again,
35 And Cæsar's eagle:[11] then his brother king,
Urien,[12] assail'd him: last a heathen horde,

[8] Power and prestige.

[9] The Round Table, according to the ancient legend, was given to Leodogran by Uther. Leodogran sent it to Arthur as a wedding gift. The table was large enough to seat 150 knights, but only 28 knights of King Arthur were found worthy to sit around it.

[10] Read the story of Romulus and Remus, mythical founders of Rome. See also Kipling's *Mowgli*.

[11] The Britons were fiercely attacked as soon as the Roman armies had been withdrawn.

[12] Urien was the husband of Morgan le Fay, sister of Arthur, and king of North Wales. Malory tells us (I. XXIV) that Urien wanted

Reddening the sun with smoke and earth with blood,
And on the spike that split the mother's heart
Spitting[13] the child, brake on him, till, amazed,[14]
He knew not whither he should turn for aid. 40

But—for he heard of Arthur newly crown'd,
Tho' not without an uproar made by those
Who cried, 'He is not Uther's son'—the King
Sent to him, saying, 'Arise, and help us thou!
For here between the man and beast we die.' 45

And Arthur yet had done no deed of arms,
But heard the call, and came: and Guinevere
Stood by the castle walls to watch him pass;
But since he neither wore on helm or shield
The golden symbol[15] of his kinglihood, 50
But rode a simple knight among his knights,
And many of these in richer arms than he,
She saw him not, or mark'd not, if she saw,
One among many, tho' his face was bare.
But Arthur, looking downward as he past, 55
Felt the light of her eyes into his life
Smite on the sudden, yet rode on, and pitch'd
His tents beside the forest. Then he drave[16]
The heathen; after, slew the beast,[17] and fell'd

Arthur's beard to complete a mantle made of the beards of kings he
had slain. Arthur finally overthrew him.

[13] A *spit* was an iron rod upon which meat was held while roasting.
[14] Confused.
[15] The *golden symbol* is described in *Lancelot and Elaine*, lines 432ff.
[16] An old form of *drove*.
[17] Beasts—wild dog, wolf, bear.

60 The forest, letting in the sun, and made
Broad pathways for the hunter and the knight
And so return'd.

             For while he linger'd there,
A doubt that ever smoulder'd in the hearts
Of those great Lords and Barons[18] of his realm
65 Flash'd forth and into war: for most of these,
Colleaguing with a score of petty kings,
Made head against him, crying: 'Who is he
That he should rule us? who hath proven him
King Uther's son? for lo! we look at him,
70 And find nor face nor bearing, limbs nor voice,
Are like to those of Uther whom we knew.
This is the son of Gorloïs,[19] not the King;
This is the son of Anton, not the King.'

     And Arthur, passing thence to battle, felt
75 Travail, and throes and agonies of the life,[20]
Desiring to be join'd with Guinevere;
And thinking as he rode, 'Her father said
That there between the man and beast they die.
Shall I not lift her from this land of beasts
80 Up to my throne, and side by side with me?
What happiness to reign a lonely king,
Vext—O ye stars that shudder over me,
O earth that soundest hollow under me,

[18] Members of the nobility who had taken their oaths to support him.

[19] Pronounced gŏr'l ō ĭs.

[20] This passage indicates the intensity of his new-born love.

Vext with waste dreams? for saving[21] I be join'd
To her that is the fairest under heaven, 85
I seem as nothing in the mighty world,
And cannot will my will, nor work my work
Wholly, nor make myself in mine own realm
Victor and lord. But were I join'd with her,
Then might we live together as one life, 90
And reigning with one will in everything
Have power on this dark land to lighten it,
And power on this dead world to make it live.'

    Thereafter—as he[22] speaks who tells the tale—
When Arthur reach'd a field-of-battle bright 95
With pitch'd pavilions[23] of his foe, the world
Was all so clear about him, that he saw
The smallest rock far on the faintest hill,
And even in high day[24] the morning star.
So when the King had set his banner broad, 100
At once from either side, with trumpet-blast,
And shouts, and clarions shrilling unto blood,[25]
The long-lanced battle[26] let their horses run.
And now the Barons and the kings prevail'd,
And now the King, as here and there that war 105
Went swaying; but the Powers who walk the world[27]

[21] Unless.
[22] Malory, author of *Le Morte d'Arthur*.
[23] Tents.
[24] At high noon.
[25] Shrill trumpets calling to the combat.
[26] Knights armed with long lances   Here *battle* is used for *battalion*, or knights in battle formation.
[27] The divinities who rule human affairs.

Made lightnings and great thunders over him,
And dazed all eyes, till Arthur by main might,
And mightier of his hands with every blow,
110 And leading all his knighthood threw[28] the kings[29]
Carádos, Urien, Cradlemont of Wales,
Claudius, and Clariance of Northumberland,
The King Brandagoras of Latangor,
With Anguisant of Erin, Morganore,
115 And Lot of Orkney. Then, before a voice
As dreadful as the shout of one who sees
To one who sins, and deems himself alone
And all the world asleep, they swerved and brake
Flying, and Arthur call'd to stay the brands[30]
120 That hack'd among the flyers, 'Ho! they yield!'
So like a painted battle the war stood
Silenced, the living quiet as the dead,
And in the heart of Arthur joy was lord.
He laugh'd upon his warrior[31] whom he loved
125 And honor'd most. 'Thou dost not doubt me King,
So well thine arm hath wrought for me to-day.'
'Sir and my liege,'[32] he cried, 'the fire of God
Descends upon thee in the battle-field:
I know thee for my King!' Whereat the two,
130 For each had warded[33] either in the fight,
Sware on the field of death a deathless love.

[28] Overthrew.

[29] Tennyson takes this list of names of the conquered kings from Malory I, VI, XIV, XV.

[30] Swords.

[31] Lancelot.

[32] Lord, or liege lord, one whom one was bound to serve exclusively.

[33] Defended.

And Arthur said, 'Man's word is God in man:[34]
Let chance what will, I trust thee to the death.'

Then quickly from the foughten field[35] he sent
Ulfius, and Brastias, and Bedivere,[36]   135
His new-made knights, to King Leodogran,
Saying, 'If I in aught have served thee well,
Give me thy daughter Guinevere to wife.'

Whom when he heard, Leodogran in heart
Debating—'How should I that am a king,   140
However much he holp[37] me at my need,
Give my one daughter saving[38] to a king,
And a king's son?'—lifted his voice, and called
A hoary man, his chamberlain,[39] to whom
He trusted all things, and of him required   145
His counsel: 'Knowest thou aught of Arthur's birth?'

Then spake the hoary chamberlain and said,
'Sir King, there be but two old men that know:
And each is twice as old as I; and one
Is Merlin,[40] the wise man that ever served   150

[34] A man's promise is sacred. See *Lancelot and Elaine*, lines 141–4.

[35] Field of battle. See *Holy Grail*, line 857.

[36] King Arthur's knights. *Bedivere* was "first made and latest left of all the knights." See *The Passing of Arthur*, line 2.

[37] Old form for *helped*.

[38] Except.

[39] Treasurer and chief counsellor, here the highest office under the king.

[40] The great magician of the Arthurian story. He was poet, soothsayer, master of all the arts, and builder of the king's harbors, ships, and halls. He was the adviser, friend, and powerful protector of the king.

King Uther thro' his magic art; and one
Is Merlin's master (so they call him) Bleys,[41]
Who taught him magic; but the scholar ran
Before[42] the master, and so far, that Bleys
155 Laid magic by, and sat him down, and wrote
All things and whatsoever Merlin did
In one great annal-book,[43] where after-years
Will learn the secret of our Arthur's birth.'

To whom the King Leodogran replied,
160 'O friend, had I been holpen half as well
By this King Arthur as by thee to-day,
Then beast and man had had their share of me:[44]
But summon here before us yet once more
Ulfius, and Brastias, and Bedivere.'

165   Then, when they came before him, the King said,
'I have seen the cuckoo chased by lesser fowl,
And reason in the chase:[45] but wherefore now
Do these your lords stir up the heat of war,
Some calling Arthur born of Gorloïs,
170 Others of Anton? Tell me, ye yourselves,
Hold ye this Arthur for King Uther's son?'

And Ulfius and Brastias answer'd, 'Ay.'
Then Bedivere, the first of all his knights

---

[41] The historian of King Arthur's time, and teacher of Merlin.

[42] Outstripped, surpassed.

[43] Chronicle book, or record of current events.

[44] Meaning, "If I had been helped as little by King Arthur as by thee, I had been badly defeated."

[45] With good reason, for cuckoos try to drive other birds from their nests.

Knighted by Arthur at his crowning, spake—
For bold in heart and act and word was he,   175
Whenever slander breathed against the King—

'Sir, there be many rumors on this head:
For there be those who hate him in their hearts,
Call him baseborn, and since his ways are sweet,
And theirs are bestial, hold him less than man: 180
And there be those who deem him more than man,
And dream he dropt from heaven: but my belief
In all this matter—so ye care to learn—
Sir, for ye know that in King Uther's time
The prince and warrior Gorloïs, he that held   185
Tintagil castle by the Cornish sea,[46]
Was wedded with a winsome wife, Ygerne:[47]
And daughters had she borne him,—one whereof,
Lot's wife, the Queen of Orkney,[48] Bellicent,
Hath ever like a loyal sister cleaved   190
To Arthur,—but a son she had not borne.
And Uther cast upon her eyes of love:
But she, a stainless wife to Gorloïs,
So loathed the bright dishonor of his love,
That Gorloïs and King Uther went to war: 195
And overthrown was Gorloïs and slain.
Then Uther in his wrath and heat besieged
Ygerne within Tintagil, where her men,
Seeing the mighty swarm about their walls,

[46] The ruins of Tintagil castle may still be seen on the coast of
Cornwall, England.

[47] As Gorloïs' wife, she was mother of Bellicent, Arthur's half sister.
As Uther's wife, she was the mother of Arthur.

[48] Queen of Orkney and Lothian in northeastern Scotland.

200 Left her and fled, and Uther enter'd in,
    And there was none to call to but himself.
    So, compass'd by the power of the King,
    Enforced she was to wed him in her tears,
    And with a shameful swiftness: afterward,
205 Not many moons, King Uther died himself,
    Moaning and wailing for an heir to rule
    After him, lest the realm should go to wrack.[49]
    And that same night, the night of the new year,
    By reason of the bitterness and grief
210 That vext[50] his mother, all before his time
    Was Arthur born, and all as soon as born
    Deliver'd at a secret postern-gate[51]
    To Merlin, to be holden far apart[52]
    Until his hour should come; because the lords
215 Of that fierce day were as the lords of this,
    Wild beasts, and surely would have torn the child
    Piecemeal among them, had they known; for each
    But sought to rule for his own self and hand,
    And many hated Uther for the sake
220 Of Gorloïs. Wherefore Merlin took the child,
    And gave him to Sir Anton, an old knight
    And ancient friend of Uther; and his wife
    Nursed the young prince, and rear'd him with her own
    And no man knew. And ever since the lords
225 Have foughten like wild beasts among themselves,
    So that the realm has gone to wrack: but now,

    [49] Ruin, wreck.
    [50] Troubled.
    [51] Rear gate.
    [52] Concealed. See also the account of Arthur's birth in lines 358–9
following.

This year, when Merlin (for his hour had come)
Brought Arthur forth, and set him in the hall,
Proclaiming, "Here is Uther's heir, your king,"
A hundred voices cried, "Away with him!   230
No king of ours! a son of Gorloïs he,
Or else the child of Anton, and no king,
Or else baseborn." Yet Merlin thro' his craft,
And while the people clamor'd for a king,
Had Arthur crown'd; but after,[53] the great lords   235
Banded,[54] and so brake out in open war.'

Then while the King debated with himself
If Arthur were the child of shamefulness,
Or born the son of Gorloïs, after death,
Or Uther's son, and born before his time,   240
Or whether there were truth in anything
Said by these three, there came to Cameliard,
With Gawain and young Modred,[55] her two sons,
Lot's wife, the Queen of Orkney, Bellicent;
Whom as he could, not as he would, the King   245
Made feast for, saying, as they sat at meat,
  'A doubtful throne is ice on summer seas.
Ye come from Arthur's court. Victor his men
Report him! Yea, but ye—think ye this king—
So many those that hate him, and so strong,   250
So few his knights, however brave they be—
Hath body enow[56] to hold his foemen down?'

[53] Afterwards.
[54] United.
[55] Pronounced gâ' wăn and mō' drĕd. Modred later proved treach-
rous to Arthur. See *The Passing of Arthur*.
[56] Forces enough.

'O King,' she cried, 'and I will tell thee: few,
Few, but all brave, all of one mind with him;
255 For I was near him when the savage yells
Of Uther's peerage[57] died, and Arthur sat
Crown'd on the daïs,[58] and his warriors cried,
"Be thou the king, and we will work thy will
Who love thee." Then the King in low deep tones,
260 And simple words of great authority,
Bound them by so strait vows[59] to his own self,
That when they rose, knighted from kneeling, some
Were pale as at the passing of a ghost,
Some flush'd, and others dazed, as one who wakes
265 Half-blinded at the coming of a light.

'But when he spake and cheer'd his Table Round
With large, divine, and comfortable words,
Beyond my tongue to tell thee—I beheld
From eye to eye thro' all their Order[60] flash
270 A momentary likeness of the King:
And ere it left their faces, thro' the cross[61]
And those around it and the Crucified,
Down from the casement over Arthur, smote
Flame-color, vert,[62] and azure, in three rays,

[57] Nobles, knights.
[58] A raised platform, at one end of the hall, upon which the king's throne usually stood.
[59] Such strict, or exacting, vows.
[60] Order of the Knights of the Round Table.
[61] A stained glass window showing the crucifixion scene, probably back of the king.
[62] Green.

ne falling upon each of three fair queens,[63]   275
Vho stood in silence near his throne, the friends
f Arthur, gazing on him, tall, with bright
weet faces, who will help him at his need.

'And there I saw mage[64] Merlin, whose vast wit
nd hundred winters are but as the hands   280
f loyal vassals[65] toiling for their liege.

'And near him stood the Lady of the Lake,[66]
Vho knows a subtler magic than his own—
lothed in white samite,[67] mystic, wonderful.
he gave the King his huge cross-hilted sword,[68]   285
Vhereby to drive the heathen out: a mist
f incense curl'd about her, and her face
Vellnigh was hidden in the minster gloom;[69]
ut there was heard among the holy hymns
voice as of the waters, for she dwells   290
own in a deep; calm, whatsoever storms
lay shake the world, and when the surface rolls,
ath power to walk the waters like our Lord.

'There likewise I beheld Excalibur[70]

[63] Referring to Malory's Queen Morgan le Fay, Arthur's sister;
ueen of Northgates; and Queen of the Wast Lands (XXI, VI). See
he Passing of Arthur, note 55.
[64] Magician.
[65] Subjects who have sworn to support their lord.
[66] The "fair damsel" who provided Arthur with his sword, Excal-
ur. See Gareth and Lynette, lines 210–24.
[67] A costly silk fabric.
[68] A sword with cross-shaped handle.
[69] The darkness of the minster, or cathedral.
[70] Arthur's sword. Pronounced ĕx kăl′ ĭ bŭr.

295 Before him at his crowning borne, the sword
That rose from out the bosom of the lake,
And Arthur row'd across and took it—rich
With jewels, elfin Urim,[71] on the hilt,
Bewildering heart and eye—the blade so bright
300 That men are blinded by it—on one side,
Graven in the oldest tongue[72] of all this world,
"Take me," but turn the blade and ye shall see,
And written in the speech ye speak yourself,
"Cast me away!" And sad was Arthur's face
305 Taking it, but old Merlin counsell'd him,
"Take thou and strike! the time to cast away
Is yet far-off." So this great brand the King
Took, and by this will beat his foemen down.'

Thereat Leodogran rejoiced, but thought
310 To sift his doubtings to the last, and ask'd,
Fixing full eyes of question on her face,
'The swallow and the swift[73] are near akin,
But thou art closer to this noble prince,
Being his own dear sister'; and she said,
315 'Daughter of Gorloïs and Ygerne am I';
'And therefore Arthur's sister?' ask'd the King.
She answer'd, 'These be secret things,' and sign'd
To those two sons to pass,[74] and let them be.
And Gawain went, and breaking into song

[71] Fairy jewels. Jewels like those worn on the breastplate of the high
priest. See *Exodus* XXVIII, 30.
[72] Engraved in Hebrew.
[73] Sometimes called the black swallow.
[74] Go out.

Sprang out, and follow'd by his flying hair   320
Ran like a colt, and leapt at all he saw:
But Modred laid his ear beside the doors,
And there half-heard; the same that afterward
Struck for the throne, and striking found his doom.

And then the Queen made answer, 'What know I?   325
For dark my mother was in eyes and hair,
And dark in hair and eyes am I; and dark
Was Gorloïs, yea and dark was Uther too,
Wellnigh to blackness; but this King is fair
Beyond the race of Britons and of men.   330
Moreover, always in my mind I hear
A cry from out the dawning of my life,
A mother weeping, and I hear her say,
'O that ye had some brother, pretty one,
To guard thee on the rough ways of the world.''' 335

'Ay,' said the King, 'and hear ye such a cry?
But when did Arthur chance upon thee first?'

'O King!' she cried, 'and I will tell thee true:
He found me first when yet a little maid:
Beaten had I been for a little fault   340
Whereof I was not guilty; and out I ran
And flung myself down on a bank of heath,[75]
And hated this fair world and all therein,
And wept, and wish'd that I were dead; and he—
I know not whether of himself he came,   345
Or brought by Merlin, who, they say, can walk

[75] Heather.

Unseen at pleasure—he was at my side,
And spake sweet words, and comforted my heart,
And dried my tears, being a child with me.
350 And many a time he came, and evermore
As I grew greater[76] grew with me; and sad
At times he seem'd, and sad with him was I,
Stern too at times, and then I loved him not,
But sweet again, and then I loved him well.
355 And now of late I see him less and less,
But those first days had golden hours for me,
For then I surely thought he would be king.

'But let me tell thee now another tale:
For Bleys, our Merlin's master, as they say,
360 Died but of late, and sent his cry[77] to me,
To hear him speak before he left his life.
Shrunk like a fairy changeling[78] lay the mage;
And when I enter'd told me that himself
And Merlin ever served about the King,
365 Uther, before he died; and on the night
When Uther in Tintagil past away
Moaning and wailing for an heir, the two
Left the still King,[79] and passing forth to breathe,
Then from the castle gateway by the chasm
370 Descending thro' the dismal night—a night
In which the bounds of heaven and earth were lost—
Beheld, so high upon the dreary deeps

[76] Older.

[77] Summons.

[78] A shrunken and shriveled child left by the fairies in place of a
beautiful one whom they have spirited away.

[79] The king still in death.

It seem'd in heaven, a ship, the shape thereof
A dragon wing'd, and all from stem to stern
Bright with a shining people on the decks,   375
And gone as soon as seen. And then the two
Dropt to the cove, and watch'd the great sea fall,
Wave after wave, each mightier than the last,
Till last, a ninth one,[80] gathering half the deep
And full of voices, slowly rose and plunged   380
Roaring, and all the wave was in a flame:
And down the wave and in the flame was borne
A naked babe, and rode[81] to Merlin's feet,
Who stoopt and caught the babe, and cried "The King!
Here is an heir for Uther!" And the fringe   385
Of that great breaker, sweeping up the strand,
Lash'd at the wizard as he spake the word,
And all at once all round him rose in fire,
So that the child and he were clothed in fire.
And presently thereafter follow'd calm,   390
Free sky[82] and stars: "And this same child," he said,
"Is he who reigns; nor could I part[83] in peace
Till this were told." And saying this the seer[84]
Went thro' the strait and dreadful pass of death,
Nor ever to be question'd any more   395
Save on the further side; but when I met
Merlin, and ask'd him if these things were truth—
The shining dragon and the naked child

[80] The ninth wave, according to a Welsh tradition, was believed to
come with far greater force than any of the others.

[81] Rode on the wave, floated.

[82] Clear Sky.

[83] Depart.

[84] Bleys, the historian, the prophet.

Descending in the glory of the seas—
400 He laugh'd as is his wont, and answer'd me
In riddling triplets[85] of old time, and said:

'"Rain, rain, and sun! a rainbow in the sky!
A young man will be wiser by and by;
An old man's wit may wander ere he die.

405 Rain, rain, and sun! a rainbow on the lea![86]
And truth is this to me, and that to thee;
And truth or clothed or[87] naked let it be.

Rain, sun, and rain! and the free blossom blows:
Sun, rain, and sun! and where is he who knows?.
410 From the great deep to the great deep he goes."[88]

'So Merlin riddling anger'd me; but thou
Fear not to give this King thine only child,
Guinevere: so great bards of him will sing
Hereafter; and dark sayings from of old
415 Ranging and ringing thro' the minds of men,
And echo'd by old folk beside their fires
For comfort after their wage-work is done,
Speak of the King; and Merlin in our time
Hath spoken also, not in jest, and sworn
420 Tho' men may wound him that he will not die,
But pass, again to come; and then or now
Utterly smite the heathen underfoot,
Till these and all men hail him for their king.'

[85] Triplets, or three rhyming lines, with double meanings.
[86] A low coastal plain.
[87] Or....or is used as *either....or*.
[88] Among the peasants in Brittany, there is still current the belief that Arthur will one day return.

She spake and King Leodogran rejoiced,
But musing 'Shall I answer yea or nay?'   425
Doubted, and drowsed, nodded and slept, and saw
Dreaming, a slope of land that ever grew,
Field after field, up to a height, the peak
Haze-hidden, and thereon a phantom king,
Now looming, and now lost; and on the slope   430
The sword rose, the hind[89] fell, the herd was driven,
Fire glimpsed; and all the land from roof and rick,[90]
In drifts of smoke before a rolling wind,
Stream'd to the peak, and mingled with the haze
And made it thicker; while the phantom king   435
Sent out at times a voice; and here or there
Stood one who pointed toward the voice, the rest
Slew on and burnt, crying, 'No king of ours,
No son of Uther, and no king of ours';
Till with a wink[91] his dream was changed, the haze   440
Descended, and the solid earth became
As nothing, but the King stood out in heaven,
Crown'd. And Leodogran awoke, and sent
Ulfius, and Brastias, and Bedivere,
Back to the court of Arthur answering yea.   445

Then Arthur charged his warrior whom he loved
And honor'd most, Sir Lancelot, to ride forth
And bring the Queen;—and watch'd him from the gates:
And Lancelot past away among the flowers,
(For then was latter April) and return'd   450
Among the flowers, in May, with Guinevere.

[89] Peasant. The peasants were slain and their herds stolen.
[90] A stack of grain.
[91] In the twinkle of an eye.

To whom arrived, by Dubric[92] the high saint,
Chief of the church in Britain, and before
The stateliest of her altar-shrines,[93] the King
455 That morn was married, while in stainless white,
The fair beginners of a nobler time,
And glorying in their vows and him, his knights
Stood round him, and rejoicing in his joy.
Far shone the fields of May thro' open door.
460 The sacred altar blossom'd white with May,
The Sun of May descended on their King,
They gazed on all earth's beauty in their Queen,
Roll'd incense, and there past along the hymns
A voice as of the waters, while the two
465 Sware at the shrine of Christ a deathless love:
And Arthur said, 'Behold, thy doom[94] is mine.
Let chance what will, I love thee to the death!'
To whom the Queen replied with drooping eyes,
'King and my lord, I love thee to the death!'
470 And holy Dubric spread his hands and spake,
'Reign ye, and live and love, and make the world
Other,[95] and may thy Queen be one with thee,
And all this Order of thy Table Round
Fulfil the boundless purpose of their King!'

475 So Dubric said; but when they left the shrine

---

[92] Primate of Britain, the papal legate, and Archbishop of Caerleon upon-Usk. A holy man who is reported as having cured many dis eases by prayer.

[93] Arthur was wedded at Camelot in the church of St. Stephens.

[94] Fortune, or fate.

[95] Better.

Great Lords from Rome[96] before the portal stood,
In scornful stillness gazing as they past;
Then while they paced a city all on fire
With sun and cloth of gold, the trumpets blew,
And Arthur's knighthood sang before the King:—   480

   'Blow trumpet, for the world is white with May;[97]
Blow trumpet, the long night hath roll'd away!
Blow thro' the living world—"Let the King reign."

   'Shall Rome or Heathen rule in Arthur's realm?
Flash brand and lance, fall battleaxe upon helm,   485
Fall battleaxe, and flash brand! Let the King reign.

   'Strike for the King and live! his knights have heard
That God hath told the King a secret word.
Fall battleaxe, and flash brand! Let the King reign.

   'Blow trumpet! he will lift us from the dust.   490
Blow trumpet! live the strength and die the lust!
Clang battleaxe, and clash brand! Let the King reign.

   'Strike for the King and die! and if thou diest,
The King is King, and ever wills the highest.
Clang battleaxe, and clash brand! Let the King reign.   495

   'Blow, for our Sun is mighty in his May!

[96] Rome had once ruled Britain and had sent these lords to collect the tribute, or taxes.

[97] Stopford A. Brooke calls this marriage and coronation song "a piece of glorious literature" and declares, "It embodies the thought of the poem, grips the whole meaning of it together."

Blow, for our Sun is mightier day by day!
Clang battleaxe, and clash brand! Let the King reign.

'The King will follow Christ, and we the King
500 In whom high God hath breathed a secret thing.[98]
Fall battleaxe, and flash brand! Let the King reign.'

So sang the knighthood, moving to their hall.
There at the banquet those great Lords from Rome,
The slowly-fading mistress of the world,[99]
505 Strode in, and claim'd their tribute[100] as of yore.
But Arthur spake, 'Behold, for these have sworn
To wage my wars, and worship me their King;
The old order changeth, yielding place to new;
And we that fight for our fair father Christ,
510 Seeing that ye be grown too weak and old
To drive the heathen from your Roman wall,
No tribute will we pay': so those great lords
Drew back in wrath, and Arthur strove with Rome.

And Arthur and his knighthood for a space[101]
515 Were all one will, and thro' that strength the King
Drew in the petty princedoms under him,
Fought, and in twelve great battles[102] overcame
The heathen hordes, and made a realm and reign'd.

[98] It was understood that Arthur was ruler by divine choice and that God would shield him to do His work.

[99] At this time, the Roman Empire was declining.

[100] A tax in return for which Rome was to protect Britain.

[101] For a time.

[102] Lancelot names these battles in *Lancelot and Elaine*, lines 284–302.

GARETH AND LYNETTE

THE last tall son of Lot and Bellicent,[1]
And tallest, Gareth, in a showerful spring
Stared at the spate.[2] A slender-shafted Pine
Lost footing, fell, and so was whirl'd away.
  'How he went down,' said Gareth, 'as a false knight 5
Or evil king before my lance if lance
Were mine to use — O senseless cataract,
Bearing all down in thy precipitancy —
And yet thou art but swollen with cold snows
And mine is living blood: thou dost His will, 10
The Maker's, and not knowest, and I that know,
Have strength and wit, in my good mother's hall
Linger with vacillating obedience,
Prison'd, and kept and coax'd and whistled to —
Since the good mother holds me still a child! 15
Good mother is bad mother unto me!
A worse were better; yet no worse would I.
Heaven yield[3] her for it, but in me put force
To weary her ears with one continuous prayer,
Until she let me fly discaged to sweep 20
In ever-highering eagle-circles up

[1] *Lot* was the crafty King of Orkney, who had betrayed King
Arthur in earlier wars. *Bellicert* was the reputed half-sister of King
Arthur.

[2] The river at flood height.

[3] Reward, or recompense.

To the great Sun of Glory, and thence swoop
Down upon all things base, and dash them dead,
A knight of Arthur, working out his will,
25 To cleanse the world. Why, Gawain,[4] when he came
With Modred[5] hither in the summertime,
Ask'd me to tilt[6] with him, the proven knight.
Modred for want of worthier was the judge.
Then I so shook him in the saddle, he said,
"Thou hast half prevail'd against me," said so —
30   he —
Tho' Modred biting his thin lips was mute,
For he is always sullen: what care I?'

And Gareth went, and hovering round her chair
Ask'd, 'Mother, tho' ye count me still the child,
35 Sweet mother, do ye love the child?' She laugh'd,
'Thou art but a wild-goose to question it.'
'Then, mother, and ye love the child,' he said,
'Being a goose and rather tame than wild,
Hear the child's story.' 'Yea, my well-beloved,
40 An[7] 'twere but of the goose and golden eggs.'[8]

And Gareth answer'd her with kindling eyes,

[4] Gawain, pronounced gô'wăn. Surnamed "The Courteous,"
eldest brother of Gareth.

[5] Modred, pronounced mō'drĕd. Second son of Lot and Bellicent,
treacherous like his father.

[6] Fight on horseback with lances.

[7] *An* is here used for *if.* See also line 50, and many instances of
similar use in later passages.

[8] The old fable of "Goose and Golden Eggs." See Tennyson's
poem, *The Goose.*

'Nay, nay, good mother, but this egg of mine
Was finer gold than any goose can lay;
For this an Eagle, a royal Eagle, laid
Almost beyond eye-reach, on such a palm   45
As glitters gilded in thy Book of Hours.[9]
And there was ever haunting round the palm
A lusty youth, but poor, who often saw
The splendour sparkling from aloft, and thought
"An I could climb and lay my hand upon it,   50
Then were I wealthier than a leash[10] of kings."
But ever when he reach'd a hand to climb,
One that had loved him from his childhood, caught
And stay'd him, "Climb not lest thou break thy neck,
I charge thee by my love" and so the boy,   55
Sweet mother, neither clomb, nor brake his neck,
And brake his very heart in pining for it,
And past away,'
        To whom the mother said,
'True love, sweet son, had risk'd himself and climb'd,
And handed down the golden treasure to him.'   60

  And Gareth answer'd her with kindling eyes,
'Gold? said I gold? — ay then, why he, or she,
Or whosoe'er it was, or half the world
Had ventured — *had* the thing I spake of been
Mere gold — but this was all of that true steel, 65
Whereof they forged the brand Excalibur,[11]

[9] A prayer-book with pictures, here one of the pictures is described.
[10] Three.
[11] *Brand* means *sword*, hence Arthur's sword Excalibur, sign of
authority, which he received from the Lady of the Lake.

And lightnings play'd about it in the storm.
And all the little fowl were flurried at it,
And there were cries and clashings in the nest,
70 That sent him from his senses: let me go.'

Then Bellicent bemoan'd herself and said,
'Hast thou no pity upon my loneliness?
Lo, where thy father Lot beside the hearth
Lies like a log, and all but smoulder'd out![12]
75 For ever since when traitor to the King
He fought against him in the Barons' war,
And Arthur gave him back his territory,
His age hath slowly droopt, and now lies there
A yet-warm corpse, and yet unburiable,
80 No more; nor sees, nor hears, nor speaks, nor knows.
And both thy brethren are in Arthur's hall,
Albeit[13] neither loved with that full love
I feel for thee, nor worthy such a love:
Stay therefore thou; red berries charm the bird,
85 And thee, mine innocent, the jousts,[14] the wars,
Who never knewest finger-ache, nor pang
Of wrench'd or broken limb — an often chance
In those brain-stunning shocks, and tourney-falls,[15]
Frights to my heart; but stay: follow the deer
90 By these tall firs and our fast-falling burns;[16]
So make thy manhood mightier day by day;

[12] All but dead.
[13] Although.
[14] The joust was a contest between knights where, in tilt and tournament, they contended for prizes, or for honor, or both.
[15] Falls which resulted from the shocks of coming together.
[16] Small rivulets, or streams.

Sweet is the chase: and I will seek thee out
Some comfortable bride and fair, to grace
Thy climbing life, and cherish my prone year,[17]
Till falling into Lot's forgetfulness   95
I know not thee, myself, nor anything.
Stay, my best son! ye are yet more boy than man.
　　Then Gareth, 'An ye hold me yet for child,
Hear yet once more the story of the child.
For, mother, there was once a King, like ours.   100
The prince his heir, when tall and marriageable,
Ask'd for a bride; thereupon the King
Set two before him. One was fair, strong, arm'd —
But to be won by force — and many men
Desired her; one, good lack,[18] no man desired,   105
And these were the conditions of the King:
That save he won the first by force, he needs
Must wed that other, whom no man desired,
A red-faced bride who knew herself so vile,
That evermore she long'd to hide herself,   110
Nor fronted[19] man or woman, eye to eye —
Yea — some she cleaved to, but they died of her.
And one — they call'd her Fame; and one,— O
　　　　mother,
How can ye keep me tether'd to you — Shame.
Man am I grown, a man's work must I do.   115
Follow the deer? follow the Christ, the King,
Live pure, speak true, right wrong, follow the King —
Else, wherefore born?'

[17] Old age.
[18] What a pity!
[19] Confronted, or faced.

To whom the mother said,
'Sweet son, for there be many who deem him not,
120 Or will not deem him, wholly proven King —[20]
Albeit in mine own heart I knew him King,
When I was frequent[21] with him in my youth,
And heard him Kingly speak, and doubted him
No more than he, himself; but felt him mine,
125 Of closest kin to me: yet — wilt thou leave
Thine easeful biding[22] here, and risk thine all,
Life, limbs, for one that is not proven King?
Stay, till the cloud that settles round his birth
Hath lifted but a little. Stay, sweet son.'

130 And Gareth answer'd quickly, 'Not an hour,
So that ye yield me — I will walk thro' fire,
Mother, to gain it — your full leave to go.
Not proven, who swept the dust of ruin'd Rome
From off the threshold of the realm, and crush'd
135 The Idolaters, and made the people free?[23]
Who should be King save him who makes us free?'

So when the Queen, who long had sought in vain
To break him from the intent to which he grew,
Found her son's will unwaveringly one,
140 She answer'd craftily, 'Will ye walk thro' fire?
Who walks thro' fire will hardly heed the smoke.

[20] Some doubt existed as to Arthur's royal birth.

[21] Often with him, or used to being with him.

[22] Easy, or comfortable surroundings.

[23] An allusion to Arthur's wars against the Romans and Saxons who invaded Britain.

Ay, go then, an ye must: only one proof,
Before thou ask the King to make thee knight,
Of thine obedience and thy love to me,
Thy mother,— I demand.'   145

                And Gareth cried,
'A hard one, or a hundred, so I go.
Nay — quick! the proof to prove me to the quick!'[24]

    But slowly spake the mother looking at him,
'Prince, thou shalt go disguised to Arthur's hall,
And hire thyself to serve for meats and drinks   150
Among the scullions and the kitchen-knaves,[25]
And those that hand the dish across the bar.[26]
Nor shalt thou tell thy name to any one.
And thou shalt serve a twelvemonth and a day.'

    For so the Queen believed that when her son   155
Beheld his only way to glory lead
Low down thro' villain kitchen-vassalage,[27]
Her own true Gareth was too princely-proud
To pass thereby; so should he rest with her,
Closed in her castle from the sound of arms.   160

    Silent awhile was Gareth, then replied,
'The thrall[28] in person may be free in soul,

---

[24] Prove me even to death.
[25] Kitchen boys.
[26] Low long table dividing the kitchen opening from the eating-room.
[27] Slavish kitchen service.
[28] Slave.

And I shall see the jousts. Thy son am I,
And since thou art my mother, must obey.
165 I therefore yield me freely to thy will;
For hence will I, disguised, and hire myself
To serve with scullions and with kitchen-knaves;
Nor tell my name to any — no, not the King.'

Gareth awhile linger'd. The mother's eye
170 Full of the wistful fear that he would go,
And turning toward him wheresoe'er he turn'd,
Perplext his outward purpose, till an hour,
When waken'd by the wind which with full voice
Swept bellowing thro' the darkness on to dawn,
175 He rose, and out of slumber calling two
That still had tended on him from his birth,[29]
Before the wakeful mother heard him, went.

The three were clad like tillers of the soil.
Southward they set their faces. The birds made
180 Melody on branch, and melody in mid air.
The damp hill-slopes were quicken'd into green,
And the live green had kindled into flowers,
For it was past the time of Easterday.

So, when their feet were planted on the plain
185 That broaden'd toward the base of Camelot,[30]
Far off they saw the silver-misty morn
Rolling her smoke about the Royal mount,
That rose between the forest and the field.

[29] His body-servants.
[30] The capital of King Arthur's realm.

At times the summit of the high city flash'd;
At times the spires and turrets half-way down   190
Prick'd thro' the mist; at times the great gate shone
Only, that open'd on the field below:
Anon, the whole fair city had disappear'd.

Then those who went with Gareth were amazed,
One crying, 'Let us go no further, lord.   195
Here is a city of Enchanters,[31] built
By fairy Kings.' The second echo'd him,
'Lord, we have heard from our wise man at home
To Northward, that this King is not the King,
But only changeling out of Fairyland,[32]   200
Who drave the heathen hence by sorcery
And Merlin's glamour.'[33] Then the first again,
'Lord, there is no such city anywhere,
But all a vision.'

                    Gareth answer'd them
With laughter, swearing he had glamour enow[34]   205
In his own blood, his princedom, youth and hopes,
To plunge old Merlin in the Arabian sea;
So push'd them all unwilling toward the gate.
And there was no gate like it under heaven.
For barefoot on the keystone, which was lined   210

[31] The attendants were overcome on approaching so wonderful a place.

[32] A hero from Fairyland.

[33] Enchantment. Merlin (mûr'lĭn) was a wonderful magician and prophet who foretold the future greatness of Britain.

[34] Enough.

And rippled like an ever-fleeting wave,
The Lady of the Lake[35] stood: all her dress
Wept from her sides as water flowing away;
But like the cross her great and goodly arms
215 Stretch'd under all the cornice and upheld:
And drops of water fell from either hand;
And down from one a sword was hung, from one
A censer, either worn with wind and storm;
And o'er her breast floated the sacred fish;
220 And in the space to left of her, and right,
Were Arthur's wars in weird devices done,
New things and old co-twisted, as if Time
Were nothing, so inveterately,[36] that men
Were giddy gazing there; and over all
225 High on the top were those three Queens, the friends
Of Arthur, who should help him at his need.

Then those with Gareth for so long a space
Stared at the figures, that at last it seem'd
The dragon-boughts[37] and elvish emblemings[38]

---

[35] *The Lady of the Lake* symbolizes religion. Her flowing dress shows that forms of religion change. Her arms supporting the cornice show that the substance of religion is unchanging. The sword stands for divine justice, the censer for worship, the sacred fish over her breast is a sign of the Christ. Arthur's wars are represented to show that strife for ideals centers about religion. The three Queens are Faith, Hope, and Love, handmaids of religion. This gateway is doubtless symbolical of the high place religion has in all right life activities.

[36] Firmly or obstinately.

[37] Dragon-tails.

[38] Figures of elves.

Began to move, seethe, twine and curl: they call'd   230
To Gareth, 'Lord, the gateway is alive.'

And Gareth likewise on them fixt his eyes
So long, that ev'n to him they seem'd to move.
Out of the city a blast of music peal'd.
Back from the gate started the three, to whom   235
From out thereunder came an ancient man,[39]
Long-bearded, saying, 'Who be ye, my sons?'

Then Gareth, 'We be tillers of the soil,
Who leaving share[40] in furrow come to see
The glories of our King: but these, my men,   240
(Your city moved so weirdly in the mist)
Doubt if the King be King at all, or come
From Fairyland; and whether this be built
By magic, and by fairy Kings and Queens;
Or whether there be any city at all,   245
Or all a vision: and this music now
Hath scared them both, but tell thou these the truth.'

Then that old Seer made answer playing on him
And saying, 'Son, I have seen the good ship sail
Keel upward, and mast downward, in the heavens,   250
And solid turrets topsy-turvy in air:[41]
And here is truth; but an it please thee not,
Take thou the truth as thou hast told it me.
For truly as thou sayest, a Fairy King

---

[39] Merlin, Arthur's teacher, and the old magician.
[40] The ploughshare.
[41] The allusion is to a mirage the old man has seen.

255 And Fairy Queens have built the city, son;
    They came from out a sacred mountain-cleft
    Toward the sunrise, each with harp in hand,
    And built it to the music of their harps.
    And, as thou sayest, it is enchanted, son,
260 For there is nothing in it as it seems
    Saving the King; tho' some there be that hold
    The King a shadow, and the city real:
    Yet take thou heed of him, for, so thou pass
    Beneath this archway, then wilt thou become
265 A thrall[42] to his enchantments, for the King
    Will bind thee by such vows, as is a shame
    A man should not be bound by, yet the which
    No man can keep; but, so thou dread to swear,
    Pass not beneath this gateway, but abide
270 Without, among the cattle of the field.
    For an ye heard a music, like enow
    They are building still, seeing the city is built
    To music, therefore never built at all,
    And therefore built for ever.'[43]

                            Gareth spake
275 Anger'd, 'Old Master, reverence thine own beard
    That looks as white as utter truth, and seems
    Wellnigh as long as thou art statured tall!
    Why mockest thou the stranger that hath been
    To thee fair-spoken?'

    [42] *Slave*, as in line 162.
    [43] Merlin's answer, though puzzling, but shows us that things are
    not what they seem. The city built to music represents civilization
    constantly changing. The King is the soul of the city binding all to
    live according to the laws of the ideal.

But the Seer replied,
'Know ye not then the Riddling of the Bards?[44]   280
"Confusion, and illusion, and relation,
Elusion, and occasion, and evasion"?
I mock thee not but as thou mockest me,
And all that see thee, for thou art not who
Thou seemest, but I know thee who thou art.   285
And now thou goest up to mock the King,
Who cannot brook[45] the shadow of any lie.'

Unmockingly the mocker ending here
Turn'd to the right, and past along the plain;
Whom Gareth looking after said, 'My men,   290
Our one white lie sits like a little ghost
Here on the threshold of our enterprise.
Let love be blamed for it, not she, nor I:
Well, we will make amends.'

With all good cheer
He spake and laugh'd, then enter'd with his twain   295
Camelot, a city of shadowy palaces.
And stately, rich in emblem and the work
Of ancient kings who did their days in stone;[46]
Which Merlin's hand, the Mage[47] at Arthur's court,
Knowing all arts, had touch'd, and everywhere   300
At Arthur's ordinance,[48] tipt with lessening peak

[44] The poet's method of speaking in riddles. The two lines following illustrate such mystic utterances.
[45] Bear or endure.
[46] Carved their stories in stone.
[47] The wise man, or master magician.
[48] According to Arthur's plan.

And pinnacle, and had made it spire to heaven.
And ever and anon a knight would pass
Outward, or inward to the hall: his arms
305 Clash'd; and the sound was good to Gareth's ear.
And out of bower and casement shyly glanced
Eyes of pure women, wholesome stars of love;
And all about a healthful people stept
As in the presence of a gracious king.

310   Then into hall Gareth ascending heard
A voice, the voice of Arthur, and beheld
Far over heads in that long-vaulted hall
The splendour of the presence of the King
Throned, and delivering doom[49]— and look'd no more—
315 But felt his young heart hammering in his ears,
And thought, 'For this half-shadow of a lie
The truthful King will doom me when I speak.'
Yet pressing on, tho' all in fear to find
Sir Gawain or Sir Modred, saw nor one
320 Nor other, but in all the listening eyes
Of those tall knights, that ranged about the throne,
Clear honour shining like the dewy star
Of dawn, and faith in their great King, with pure
Affection, and the light of victory,
325 And glory gain'd, and evermore to gain.

Then came a widow crying to the King,
'A boon, Sir King! Thy father, Uther, reft[50]

[49] Pronouncing judgment on cases brought before him. See also
line 317.
[50] Took.

From my dead lord a field with violence:
For howsoe'er at first he proffer'd gold,
Yet, for the field was pleasant in our eyes, 380
We yielded not; and then he reft us of it
Perforce, and left us neither gold nor field.'

Said Arthur, 'Whether would ye? gold or field?'
To whom the woman weeping, 'Nay, my lord,
The field was pleasant in my husband's eye.' 385

And Arthur, 'Have thy pleasant field again,
And thrice the gold for Uther's use thereof,
According to the years. No boon[51] is here,
But justice, so thy say be proven true.
Accursed, who from the wrongs his father did 340
Would shape himself a right!'[52]

                              And while she past,
Came yet another widow crying to him,
A boon, Sir King! Thine enemy, King, am I.
With thine own hand thou slewest my dear lord,
A knight of Uther in the Barons' war, 345
When Lot and many another rose and fought
Against thee, saying thou wert basely born.
I held with these, and loathe to ask thee aught.
Yet lo! my husband's brother had my son
Thrall'd in his castle, and hath starved him dead; 350
And standeth seized[53] of that inheritance

---

[51] Reward, or bonus.
[52] Arthur condemns rights acquired through injustice.
[53] Is in possession of.

Which thou that slewest the sire hast left the son.
So tho' I scarce can ask it thee for hate,
Grant me some knight to do the battle for me,
355 Kill the foul thief, and wreak[54] me for my son.'

Then strode a good knight forward, crying to him,
'A boon, Sir King! I am her kinsman, I.
Give me to right her wrong, and slay the man.'

Then came Sir Kay,[55] the seneschal, and cried,
360 'A boon, Sir King! ev'n that thou grant her none,
This railer, that hath mock'd thee in full hall—
None; or the wholesome boon of gyve and gag.'[56]

But Arthur, 'We sit King, to help the wrong'd
Thro' all our realm. The woman loves her lord.
365 Peace to thee, woman, with thy loves and hates!
The kings of old had doom'd thee to the flames,
Aurelius Emrys[57] would have scourged thee dead,
And Uther slit thy tongue: but get thee hence —
Lest that rough humour[58] of the kings of old
370 Return upon me! Thou that art her kin,
Go likewise; lay him low and slay him not,
But bring him here, that I may judge the right,
According to the justice of the King:

[54] Avenge.

[55] Arthur's steward, blunt, rough, but faithful.

[56] The favor of fetters, or chains, and a gag to keep her loud mouth shut.

[57] The last in the line of Roman Emperors in Britain, succeeded by Uther, father of Arthur.

[58] Mood.

Then, be he guilty, by that deathless King[59]
Who lived and died for men, the man shall die.'   375

Then came in hall the messenger of Mark,[60]
A name of evil savour in the land,
The Cornish king. In either hand he bore
What dazzled all, and shone far-off as shines
A field of charlock[61] in the sudden sun   380
Between two showers, a cloth of palest gold,
Which down he laid before the throne, and knelt,
Delivering,[62] that his lord, the vassal[63] king,
Was ev'n upon his way to Camelot;
For having heard that Arthur of his grace   385
Had made his goodly cousin, Tristram, knight,
And, for himself was of the greater state,
Being a king, he trusted his liege-lord
Would yield him this large honour all the more;
So pray'd him well to accept this cloth of gold,   390
In token of true heart and fealty.[64]

Then Arthur cried to rend the cloth, to rend
In pieces, and so cast it on the hearth.
An oak-tree smoulder'd there. 'The goodly knight!
What! shall the shield of Mark stand among these?'   395
For, midway down the side of that long hall

[59] Christ.
[60] Wicked King of Cornwall.
[61] Yellow wild mustard.
[62] Saying in formal manner.
[63] A subject king who had sworn loyalty to Arthur in return for
lands granted.
[64] Loyalty.

A stately pile,[65]— whereof along the front,
Some blazon'd,[66] some but carven,[67] and some blank,
There ran a treble range of stony shields,—
400 Rose, and high-arching overbrow'd[68] the hearth.
And under every shield a knight was named:
For this was Arthur's custom in his hall;
When some good knight had done one noble deed,
His arms were carven only; but if twain
405 His arms were blazon'd also; but if none,
The shield was blank and bare without a sign
Saving the name beneath; and Gareth saw
The shield of Gawain blazon'd rich and bright,
And Modred's blank as death; and Arthur cried
410 To rend the cloth and cast it on the hearth.

'More like are we to reave[69] him of his crown
Than make him knight because men call him king.
The kings we found, ye know we stay'd their hands
From war among themselves, but left them kings;
415 Of whom were any bounteous, merciful,
Truth-speaking, brave, good livers, them we enroll'd
Among us, and they sit within our hall.
But Mark hath tarnish'd the great name of king,
As Mark would sully the low state of churl:[70]
420 And, seeing he hath sent us cloth of gold,

---

[65] Hall, or building.
[66] Marked with the coat of arms, or family emblem, in colors.
[67] The coat of arms was carved without coloring.
[68] Hung over.
[69] Take from, an old form of *bereave*.
[70] Mark was unworthy to be even a peasant.

Return, and meet, and hold him from our eyes,
Lest we should lap[71] him up in cloth of lead,
Silenced for ever — craven[72] — a man of plots,
Crafts, poisonous counsels, wayside ambushings[73]—
No fault of thine: let Kay the seneschal   425
Look to thy wants, and send thee satisfied —
Accursed, who strikes nor lets the hand be seen!'

And many another suppliant crying came
With noise[74] of ravage wrought by beast and man,
And evermore a knight would ride away.   430

Last, Gareth leaning both hands heavily
Down on the shoulders of the twain, his men,
Approach'd between them toward the King, and ask'd,
A boon, Sir King (his voice was all ashamed),
For see ye not how weak and hungerworn   435
I seem — leaning on these? grant me to serve
For meat and drink among thy kitchen-knaves
A twelvemonth and a day, nor seek my name.
Hereafter I will fight.'

                    To him the King,
A goodly youth and worth a goodlier boon!   440
But so thou wilt no goodlier, then must Kay,
The master of the meats and drinks, be thine.'

[71] Wrap. Sheet-lead was once wrapped about dead bodies to pre-
pare them for burial.
[72] Coward.
[73] An intriguing, crafty, lying, treacherous one, and hence unworthy
knighthood.
[74] Complaint.

He rose and past; then Kay, a man of mien
Wan-sallow[75] as the plant that feels itself
445 Root-bitten by white lichen,

               'Lo ye now!
This fellow hath broken from some Abbey,[76] where,
God wot, he had not beef and brewis[77] enow,
However that might chance! but an he work,
Like any pigeon will I cram his crop,
450 And sleeker shall he shine than any hog.'

Then Lancelot standing near, 'Sir Seneschal,[78]
Sleuth-hound[79] thou knowest, and gray, and all the
           hounds;
A horse thou knowest, a man thou dost not know:
Broad brows and fair, a fluent hair and fine,
455 High nose, a nostril large and fine, and hands
Large, fair and fine!— Some young lad's mystery —
But, or from sheepcot or[80] king's hall, the boy
Is noble-natured. Treat him with all grace
Lest he should come to shame thy judging of him.'

460   Then Kay, 'What murmurest thou of mystery?
Think ye this fellow will poison the King's dish?[81]

[75] A man of pale, wan appearance.

[76] A monastery where the monks live.

[77] "Bread soaked in broth"—*Webster*.

[78] The master of the King's palace.

[79] Blood-hound.

[80] *Whether* from the sheepcot *or*.

[81] In olden times, there was constant danger that kitchen attendants might be bribed to poison the king's food.

ay, for he spake too fool-like: mystery!
ut, an the lad were noble, he had ask'd
or horse and armour: fair and fine, forsooth!
ir Fine-face, Sir Fair-hands? but see thou to it   465
'hat thine own fineness, Lancelot, some fine day
ndo thee not — and leave my man to me.'

  So Gareth all for glory underwent
'he sooty yoke of kitchen-vassalage;
te with young lads his portion by the door,   470
nd couch'd[82] at night with grimy kitchen-knaves.
nd Lancelot ever spake him pleasantly,
.t Kay the seneschal, who loved him not,
Vould hustle and harry[83] him, and labour him
eyond his comrade of the hearth, and set   475
'o turn the broach,[84] draw water, or hew wood,
'r grosser tasks; and Gareth bow'd himself
Vith all obedience to the King, and wrought
ll kind of service with a noble ease
'hat graced the lowliest act in doing it.   480
nd when the thralls had talk among themselves,
nd one would praise the love that linkt the King
nd Lancelot — how the King had saved his life
n battle twice, and Lancelot once the King's —
or Lancelot was the first in Tournament,[85]   485
ut Arthur mightiest on the battle-field —
areth was glad. Or if some other told,

[82] Slept.
[83] Annoy.
[84] Set him to turn the spit for roasting meats.
[85] The great gathering where knights contended for honors.

How once the wandering forester at dawn,
Far over the blue tarns[86] and hazy seas,
490 On Caer-Eryri's highest[87] found the King,
A naked babe, of whom the Prophet spake,
'He passes to the Isle Avilion,[88]
He passes and is heal'd and cannot die'—
Gareth was glad. But if their talk were foul,
495 Then would he whistle rapid as any lark,
Or carol some old roundelay,[89] and so loud
That first they mock'd, but, after, reverenced him.
Or Gareth telling some prodigious tale
Of knights, who sliced a red life-bubbling way
500 Thro' twenty folds of twisted dragon, held
All in a gap-mouth'd circle his good mates
Lying or sitting round him, idle hands,
Charm'd; till Sir Kay, the seneschal, would come
Blustering upon them, like a sudden wind
505 Among dead leaves, and drive them all apart.
Or when the thralls had sport among themselves,
So there were any trial of mastery,
He, by two yards in casting bar or stone
Was counted best; and if there chanced a joust,
510 So that Sir Kay nodded him leave to go,
Would hurry thither, and when he saw the knights
Clash like the coming and retiring wave,
And the spear spring, and good horse reel, the boy
Was half beyond himself for ecstasy.

[86] Mountain lakes.
[87] Snowdon, highest peak of Britain.
[88] The Earthly Paradise of the Britains.
[89] Melody.

So for a month he wrought among the thralls;   515
ut in the weeks that follow'd, the good Queen,[90]
epentant of the word she made him swear,
nd saddening in her childless castle, sent,
etween the in-crescent and de-crescent moon,[91]
rms for her son, and loosed him from his vow.   520

This, Gareth hearing from a squire[92] of Lot
ith whom he used to play at tourney once,
hen both were children, and in lonely haunts
ould scratch a ragged oval on the sand,
nd each at either dash from either end —   525
ame never made girl redder than Gareth joy.
e laugh'd; he sprang. 'Out of the smoke, at once
leap from Satan's foot to Peter's knee[93]—
hese news be mine, none other's — nay, the King's —
escend into the city:' whereon he sought   530
he King alone, and found, and told him all.

'I have stagger'd thy strong Gawain in a tilt
or pastime; yea, he said it: joust can I.
[ake me thy knight — in secret! let my name
e hidd'n, and give me the first quest,[94] I spring   535
ke flame from ashes.'

            Here the King's calm eye
ell on, and check'd, and made him flush, and bow

[90] Queen Bellicent.
[91] Between the new moon and the full.
[92] An attendant, or armor-bearer, of a knight.
[93] From hell to heaven.
[94] Adventure, or commission to do, perform a deed of valor for the
ng.

Lowly, to kiss his hand, who answer'd him,
'Son, the good mother let me know thee here,
540 And sent her wish that I would yield thee thine.
Make thee my knight? my knights are sworn to vows
Of utter hardihood,[95] utter gentleness,
And, loving, utter faithfulness in love,
And uttermost obedience to the King.'

545   Then Gareth, lightly springing from his knees,
'My King, for hardihood I can promise thee.
For uttermost obedience make demand
Of whom ye gave me to, the Seneschal,
No mellow master of the meats and drinks!
550 And as for love, God wot,[96] I love not yet,
But love I shall, God willing.'

                              And the King —
'Make thee my knight in secret? yea, but he,
Our noblest brother, and our truest man,
And one with me in all, he needs must know.'

555   'Let Lancelot know, my King, let Lancelot know,
Thy noblest and thy truest!'

                              And the King —
'But wherefore would ye men should wonder at you?
Nay, rather for the sake of me, their King,
And the deed's sake my knighthood do the deed,
560 Than to be noised of.'

    [95] Bravery.
    [96] Knows.

            Merrily Gareth ask'd,
Have I not earn'd my cake in baking of it?
Let be my name until I make my name!
My deeds will speak: it is but for a day.'
So with a kindly hand on Gareth's arm
Smiled the great King, and half-unwillingly   565
Loving his lusty youthhood yielded to him.
Then, after summoning Lancelot privily,[97]
'I have given him the first quest: he is not proven.
Look therefore when he calls for this in hall,
Thou get to horse and follow him far away.   570
Cover the lions on thy shield, and see
Far as thou mayest, he be nor ta'en nor slain.'

    Then that same day there past into the hall
A damsel of high lineage, and a brow
May-blossom,[98] and a cheek of apple-blossom,   575
Hawk-eye; and lightly was her slender nose
Tip-tilted like the petal of a flower;
She into hall past with her page and cried,

    'O King, for thou hast driven the foe without,
See to the foe within! bridge, ford, beset   580
By bandits, everyone that owns a tower
The Lord for half a league. Why sit ye there?
Rest would I not, Sir King, an I were king,
Till ev'n the lonest hold[99] were all as free
From cursed bloodshed, as thine altar-cloth   585

[97] Privately.
[98] A brow like the pure, white hawthorn flowers.
[99] Household, or dwelling.

From that best blood[100] it is a sin to spill.'

'Comfort thyself,' said Arthur, 'I nor mine
Rest: so my knighthood keep the vows they swore,
The wastest moorland of our realm shall be
590 Safe, damsel, as the centre of this hall.
What is thy name? thy need?'

                             'My name?' she said—
'Lynette my name; noble; my need, a knight,
To combat for my sister, Lyonors,
A lady of high lineage, of great lands,
595 And comely, yea, and comelier than myself.
She lives in Castle Perilous: a river
Runs in three loops about her living place;
And o'er it are three passings,[101] and three knights
Defend the passings, brethren, and a fourth
600 And of that four the mightiest, holds her stayed[102]
In her own castle, and so besieges her
To break her will, and make her wed with him:
And but delays his purport[103] till thou send
To do the battle with him, thy chief man
605 Sir Lancelot whom he trusts to overthrow,
Then wed, with glory: but she will not wed
Save whom she loveth, or a holy life.[104]
Now therefore have I come for Lancelot.'

Then Arthur mindful of Sir Gareth ask'd,

[100] Wine of the holy sacrament.
[101] Passageways.
[102] Imprisoned.
[103] Delays carrying out his plan.
[104] She will become a nun rather than wed a man she does not love.

Damsel, ye know this Order[105] lives to crush   610
All wrongers of the Realm. But say, these four,
Who be they? What the fashion of the men?'

'They be of foolish fashion, O Sir King,
The fashion of that old knight-errantry[106]
Who ride abroad, and do but what they will;   615
Courteous or bestial from the moment, such
As have nor law nor king; and three of these
Proud in their fantasy call themselves the Day,
Morning-Star, and Noon-Sun, and Evening-Star,
Being strong fools; and never a whit more wise   620
The fourth, who always rideth arm'd in black,
A huge man-beast of boundless savagery.
He names himself the Night and oftener Death,
And wears a helmet mounted with a skull,
And bears a skeleton figured on his arms,   625
To show that who may slay or scape the three,
Slain by himself, shall enter endless night.
And all these four be fools, but mighty men,
And therefore am I come for Lancelot.'

Hereat Sir Gareth call'd from where he rose,   630
His head with kindling eyes above the throng,
'A boon, Sir King — this quest!' then — for he mark'd

---

[105] The Order of the Round Table, founded by Arthur to bring
together the strong knights of his realm and to bind them by vows
of obedience, Christianity, truth, love, and courage. The full number of seats at the Round Table was one hundred fifty.
[106] The old knights who wandered about and lived on the principle
that "Might makes right."

Kay near him groaning like a wounded bull —
'Yea, King, thou knowest thy kitchen-knave am I,
635 And mighty thro' thy meats and drinks am I,
And I can topple over a hundred such.
Thy promise, King,' and Arthur glancing at him,
Brought down a momentary brow:[107] 'Rough, sudden
And pardonable, worthy to be knight —
640 Go therefore,' and all hearers were amazed.

But on the damsel's forehead shame, pride, wrath
Slew the May-white:[108] she lifted either arm,
'Fie on thee, King! I ask'd for thy chief knight,
And thou hast given me but a kitchen-knave.'
645 Then ere a man in hall could stay her, turn'd,
Fled down the lane of access to the King,
Took horse, descended the slope street, and past
The weird white gate, and paused without, beside
The field of tourney, murmuring 'kitchen-knave.'

650   Now two great entries open'd from the hall,
At one end one that gave upon a range
Of level pavement where the King would pace
At sunrise, gazing over plain and wood;
And down from this a lordly stairway sloped
655 Till lost in blowing trees and tops of towers;
And out by this main doorway past the King.
But one was counter[109] to the hearth, and rose
High that the highest-crested helm could ride

107 Frowned.
108 The blush of anger replaced the pure white of her brow.
109 Opposite.

herethro' nor graze: and by this entry fled
he damsel in her wrath, and on to this   660
ir Gareth strode, and saw without the door
ing Arthur's gift, the worth of half a town,
warhorse of the best, and near it stood
he two that out of north had follow'd him:
his bare a maiden shield,[110] a casque;[111] that held   665
he horse, the spear; whereat Sir Gareth loosed
cloak that dropt from collar-bone to heel,
cloth of roughest web, and cast it down,
nd from it like a fuel-smother'd fire,
hat lookt half-dead, brake bright, and flash'd as those   670
ull-coated things,[112] that making slide apart
heir dusk wing-cases, all beneath there burns
jewell'd harness, ere they pass and fly.
o Gareth ere he parted flash'd in arms.
hen as he donn'd[113] the helm, and took the shield   675
nd mounted horse and graspt a spear, of grain[114]
torm-strengthen'd on a windy site, and tipt
ith trenchant[115] steel, around him slowly prest
he people, while from out of kitchen came
he thralls in throng, and seeing who had work'd   680
ustier than any, and whom they could but love,
ounted in arms, threw up their caps and cried,
God bless the King, and all his fellowship!'

[110] A blank shield.
[111] A helmet.
[112] An allusion to the beetle about to fly.
[113] Put on.
[114] A spear of tough grain, or fibre.
[115] Sharp.

And on thro' lanes of shouting Gareth rode
635 Down the slope street, and past without the gate.

So Gareth past with joy; but as the cur
Pluckt from the cur he fights with, ere his cause
Be cool'd by fighting, follows, being named,
His owner, but remembers all, and growls
690 Remembering, so Sir Kay beside the door
Mutter'd in scorn of Gareth whom he used
To harry and hustle.

     'Bound upon a quest
With horse and arms — the King hath past his time —
My scullion knave! Thralls to your work again,
695 For an your fire be low ye kindle mine!
Will there be dawn in West and eve in East?
Begone!— my knave!— belike and like enow
Some old head-blow[116] not heeded in his youth
So shook his wits they wander in his prime —
700 Crazed! How the villain lifted up his voice,
Nor shamed to bawl himself a kitchen-knave.
Tut: he was tame and meek enow with me,
Till peacock'd[117] up with Lancelot's noticing.
Well — I will after my loud knave, and learn
705 Whether he know me for his master yet.
Out of the smoke he came, and so my lance
Hold, by God's grace, he shall into the mire —
Thence, if the King awaken from his craze,
Into the smoke again.'

[116] Kay explains the King's action on the theory of a mind u
balanced either by old age or by an accident in youth.

[117] Made vain or over proud.

But Lancelot said,
Kay, wherefore wilt thou go against the King,   710
'or that did never he whereon ye rail,
But ever meekly served the King in thee?
Abide: take counsel; for this lad is great
And lusty, and knowing both of lance and sword.'
'Tut, tell not me,' said Kay, 'ye are overfine   715
To mar stout knaves with foolish courtesies:'
Then mounted, on thro' silent faces rode
Down the slope city, and out beyond the gate.

But by the field of tourney lingering yet
Mutter'd the damsel, 'Wherefore did the King   720
Scorn me? for, were Sir Lancelot lackt,[118] at least
He might have yielded to me one of those
Who tilt for lady's love and glory here,
Rather than — O sweet heaven! O fie upon him —
His kitchen-knave.'   725

To whom Sir Gareth drew
(And there were none but few[119] goodlier than he)
Shining in arms, 'Damsel, the quest is mine.
Lead, and I follow.' She thereat, as one
That smells a foul-flesh'd agaric in the holt,[120]
And deems it carrion of some woodland thing,   730
Or shrew, or weasel, nipt her slender nose
With petulant thumb and finger, shrilling, 'Hence!

[118] Not granted.
[119] There were but few, or only a few.
[120] A poisonous toadstool in the woods.

Avoid, thou smellest all of kitchen-grease.
And look who comes behind,' for there was Kay.
735 'Knowest thou not me? thy master? I am Kay.
We lack thee by the hearth.'

                      And Gareth to him,
'Master no more! too well I know thee, ay —
The most ungentle knight in Arthur's hall.'
  'Have at thee then,' said Kay: they shock'd[121] and Ka
740 Fell shoulder-slipt,[122] and Gareth cried again,
'Lead, and I follow,' and fast away she fled.

But after sod and shingle[123] ceased to fly
Behind her, and the heart of her good horse
Was nigh to burst with violence of the beat,
745 Perforce she stay'd, and overtaken spoke.

  'What doest thou, scullion, in my fellowship?
Deem'st thou that I accept thee aught the more
Or love thee better, that by some device
Full cowardly, or by mere unhappiness,
750 Thou has overthrown and slain thy master — thou!—
Dish-washer and broach-turner, loon![124]— to me
Thou smellest all of kitchen as before.'

  'Damsel,' Sir Gareth answer'd gently, 'say
Whate'er ye will, but whatsoe'er ye say,
755 I leave not till I finish this fair quest,
Or die therefore.'

---

121 Rushed together, spears pointed at each other.
122 Shoulder dislocated.
123 Coarse gravel.   124 Spit-turner and fool.

                    'Ay, wilt thou finish it?
sweet lord, how like a noble knight he talks!
The listening rogue hath caught the manner of it.
But, knave, anon thou shalt be met with, knave,   760
And then by such a one that thou for all
The kitchen brewis that was ever supt
Shalt not once dare to look him in the face.'

    'I shall assay,'[125] said Gareth with a smile
That madden'd her, and away she flash'd again
Down the long avenues of a boundless wood,   765
And Gareth following was again beknaved.[126]

    'Sir Kitchen-knave, I have miss'd the only way
Where Arthur's men are set along the wood;
The wood is nigh as full of thieves as leaves:
If both be slain, I am rid of thee; but yet,   770
Sir Scullion, canst thou use that spit of thine?
Fight, an thou canst: I have miss'd the only way.'

    So till the dusk that follow'd even-song[127]
Rode on the two, reviler and reviled;
Then after one long slope was mounted, saw,   775
Bowl-shaped, thro' tops of many thousand pines
A gloomy-gladed hollow slowly sink
To westward — in the deeps whereof a mere,[128]
Round as the red eye of an Eagle-owl,[129]

[125] Try, or attempt the quest as granted by the King.
[126] Made to feel like a kitchen attendant.
[127] The time for vespers, or evening service.
[128] Lake.
[129] The great horned owl.

780 Under the half-dead sunset glared; and shouts
Ascended, and there brake a serving man
Flying from out of the black wood, and crying,
'They have bound my lord to cast him in the mere.'
Then Gareth, 'Bound am I to right the wrong'd,
785 But straitlier bound am I to bide with thee.'
And when the damsel spake contemptuously,
'Lead, and I follow,' Gareth cried again,
'Follow, I lead!' so down among the pines
He plunged; and there, blackshadow'd nigh the mere,
790 And mid-thigh-deep in bulrushes and reed,
Saw six tall men haling[130] a seventh along,
A stone about his neck to drown him in it.
Three with good blows he quieted, but three,
Fled thro' the pines; and Gareth loosed the stone
795 From off his neck, then in the mere beside
Tumbled it; oilily bubbled up the mere.
Last, Gareth loosed his bonds and on free feet
Set him, a stalwart Baron, Arthur's friend.

'Well that ye came, or else these caitiff rogues[131]
800 Had wreak'd themselves[132] on me; good cause is their
To hate me, for my wont[133] hath ever been
To catch my thief, and then like vermin here
Drown him, and with a stone about his neck;
And under this wan water many of them
805 Lie rotting, but at night let go the stone,

[130] Dragging.
[131] Wicked rogues.
[132] Worked their vengeance.
[133] Custom.

nd rise, and flickering in a grimly light[134]
ance on the mere.   Good now, ye have saved a life
Vorth somewhat as the cleanser of this wood.
nd fain would I reward thee worshipfully.
Vhat guerdon[135] will ye?'   810

                              Gareth sharply spake,
None! for the deed's sake have I done the deed,
n uttermost obedience to the King.
ut wilt thou yield this damsel harbourage?'[136]

Whereat the Baron saying, 'I well believe
ou be of Arthur's Table,' a light laugh   81I
roke from Lynette, 'Ay, truly of a truth,
nd in a sort, being Arthur's kitchen-knave!—
ut deem not I accept thee aught the more,
cullion, for running sharply with thy spit
own on a rout of craven foresters.   82I
thresher with his flail had scatter'd them.
ay — for thou smellest of the kitchen still.
ut an this lord will yield us harbourage, well.'

So she spake.   A league beyond the wood,
ll in a full-fair manor[137] and a rich,   82I
is towers where that day a feast had been
eld in high hall, and many a viand[138] left,

[134] Ghost-like light.
[135] What reward do you want?
[136] Food and shelter.
[137] A rich nobleman's landed estate.
[138] Provision.

And many a costly cate,[139] received the three.
And there they placed a peacock in his pride[140]
830 Before the damsel, and the Baron set
Gareth beside her, but at once she rose.

'Meseems, that here is much discourtesy,
Setting this knave, Lord Baron, at my side.
Hear me — this morn I stood in Arthur's hall,
835 And pray'd the King would grant me Lancelot
To fight the brotherhood of Day and Night —
The last a monster unsubduable
Of any save of him for whom I call'd —
Suddenly bawls this frontless[141] kitchen-knave,
840 "The quest is mine; thy kitchen-knave am I,
And mighty thro' thy meats and drinks.
Then Arthur all at once gone mad replies,
"Go therefore," and so gives the quest to him —
Him — here — a villain fitter to stick swine
845 Than ride abroad redressing woman's wrong,
Or sit beside a noble gentlewoman.'

Then half-ashamed and part-amazed, the lord
Now look'd at one and now at other, left
The damsel by the peacock in his pride,
850 And, seating Gareth at another board,
Sat down beside him, ate and then began.

[139] Food delicacy.
[140] A roasted peacock was served as a special delicacy. Before
Knights renewed their vows of courage, and ladies promised to
loving and true.
[141] Bold, presumptuous.

'Friend, whether thou be kitchen-knave, or not,
Or whether it be the maiden's fantasy,
And whether she be mad, or else the King,
Or both or neither, or thyself be mad,   856
I ask not: but thou strikest a strong stroke,
For strong thou art and goodly therewithal,
And saver of my life; and therefore now,
For here be mighty men to joust with, weigh
Whether thou wilt not with thy damsel back   860
To crave again Sir Lancelot of the King.
Thy pardon; I but speak for thine avail,
The saver of my life.'[142]

               And Gareth said,
'Full pardon, but I follow up the quest,
Despite of Day and Night and Death and Hell.'   865

So when, next morn, the lord whose life he saved
Had, some brief space, convey'd them on their way
And left them with God-speed, Sir Gareth spake,
'Lead, and I follow.' Haughtily she replied,

'I fly no more: I allow thee for an hour.   870
Lion and stoat[143] have isled together, knave,
In time of flood. Nay, furthermore, methinks
Some ruth[144] is mine for thee. Back wilt thou, fool?
For hard by here is one will overthrow

[142] The host shows real knightly courtesy.
[143] The lion and the tiny weasel have lived together when forced
to do so.
[144] Some pity is due thee.

875 And slay thee: then will I to court again,
   And shame the King for only yielding me
   My champion from the ashes of his hearth.'

   To whom Sir Gareth answer'd courteously,
   'Say thou thy say, and I will do my deed.
880 Allow me for mine hour, and thou wilt find
   My fortunes all as fair as hers who lay
   Among the ashes and wedded the King's son.'[145]

   Then to the shore of one of those long loops
   Wherethro' the serpent river coil'd, they came.
885 Rough-thicketed were the banks and steep; the stream
   Full, narrow; this a bridge of single arc
   Took at a leap; and on the further side
   Arose a silk pavilion, gay with gold
   In streaks and rays, and all Lent-lily[146] in hue,
890 Save that the dome was purple, and above,
   Crimson, a slender banneret[147] fluttering.
   And therebefore the lawless warrior paced
   Unarm'd, and calling, 'Damsel, is this he,
   The champion thou hast brought from Arthur's hall?
895 For whom we let thee pass.' 'Nay, nay,' she said,
   'Sir Morning-Star. The King in utter scorn
   Of thee and thy much folly hath sent thee here
   His kitchen-knave: and look thou to thyself:
   See that he fall not on thee suddenly,
900 And slay thee unarm'd: he is not knight but knave.'

[145] An allusion to Cinderella.
[146] Daffodil.
[147] A small banner of knighthood.

Then at his call, 'O daughters of the Dawn,
And servants of the Morning-Star, approach,
Arm me,' from out the silken curtain-folds
Bare-footed and bare-headed three fair girls
In gilt and rosy raiment came: their feet   905
In dewy grasses glisten'd; and the hair
All over glanced with dewdrop or with gem
Like sparkles in the stone Avanturine.[148]
These arm'd him in blue arms, and gave a shield
Blue also, and thereon the morning star.   910
And Gareth silent gazed upon the knight,
Who stood a moment, ere his horse was brought,
Glorying; and in the stream beneath him, shone
Immingled with Heaven's azure waveringly,
The gay pavilion and the naked feet,   915
His arms, the rosy raiment, and the star.

Then she that watch'd him, 'Wherefore stare ye so?
Thou shakest in thy fear: there yet is time:
Flee down the valley before he get to horse.
Who will cry shame?   Thou art not knight but knave.'   920

Said Gareth, 'Damsel, whether knave or knight,
Far liefer had I fight a score of times
Then hear thee so missay[149] me and revile.
Fair words were best for him who fights for thee;
But truly foul are better, for they send   925
That strength of anger thro' mine arms, I know
That I shall overthrow him.'

[148] A variety of quartz with flakes of mica or other minerals.
[149] Misinterpret.

                                        And he that bore
The star, then mounted, cried from o'er the bridge,
'A kitchen-knave, and sent in scorn of me!
930 Such fight not I, but answer scorn with scorn.
For this were shame to do him further wrong
Than set him on his feet, and take his horse
And arms, and so return him to the King.
Come, therefore, leave thy lady lightly, knave.
935 Avoid: [150] for it beseemeth not a knave
To ride with such a lady.'

                                        'Dog, thou liest.
I spring from loftier lineage than thine own.'
He spake; and all at fiery speed the two
Shock'd on the central bridge, and either spear
940 Bent but not brake, and either knight at once,
Hurl'd as a stone from out of a catapult [151]
Beyond his horse's crupper and the bridge,
Fell, as if dead; but quickly rose and drew,
And Gareth lash'd so fiercely with his brand
945 He drave his enemy backward down the bridge,
The damsel crying, 'Well-stricken, kitchen-knave!'
Till Gareth's shield was cloven; but one stroke
Laid him that clove it grovelling on the ground.

    Then cried the fall'n, 'Take not my life: I yield.'
950 And Gareth, 'So this damsel ask it of me
Good — I accord it easily as a grace.' [152]

    [150] Dismount and cease your quest.
    [151] An ancient machine used in war to throw stones into walled
cities or against foes.
    [152] Grace, a favor.

She reddening, 'Insolent scullion: I of thee?
I bound to thee for any favour ask'd!'
'Then shall he die.' And Gareth there unlaced
His helmet as to slay him, but she shriek'd,   955
'Be not so hardy, scullion, as to slay
One nobler than thyself.' 'Damsel, thy charge[153]
Is an abounding pleasure to me. Knight,
Thy life is thine at her command. Arise
And quickly pass to Arthur's hall, and say   960
His kitchen-knave hath sent thee. See thou crave
His pardon for thy breaking of his laws.
Myself, when I return, will plead for thee.
Thy shield is mine — farewell; and, damsel, thou,
Lead, and I follow.'   965

           And fast away she fled.
Then when he came upon her, spake, 'Methought,
Knave, when I watch'd thee striking on the bridge
The savour of thy kitchen came upon me
A little faintlier: but the wind hath changed:
I scent it twenty-fold.' And then she sang,   970
'"O morning star" (not that tall felon there
Whom thou by sorcery or unhappiness[154]
Or some device, hast foully[155] overthrown),
"O morning star that smilest in the blue,
O star, my morning dream hath proven true,   975
Smile sweetly, thou! my love hath smiled on me."

[153] Request. A true knight would not slay an enemy if a lady
requested that the enemy's life be spared.
[154] Misfortune, or mischance.
[155] Overthrown unfairly.

'But thou begone, take counsel, and away,
For hard by here is one that guards a ford —
The second brother in their fool's parable[156]—
980 Will pay thee all thy wages, and to boot.
Care not for shame: thou art not knight but knave.'

To whom Sir Gareth answer'd laughingly,
'Parables? Hear a parable of the knave.
When I was kitchen-knave among the rest
985 Fierce was the hearth, and one of my co-mates
Own'd a rough dog, to whom he cast his coat,
"Guard it," and there was none to meddle with it.
And such a coat art thou, and thee the King
Gave me to guard, and such a dog am I,
990 To worry, and not to flee — and — knight or knave —
The knave that doth thee service as full knight
Is all as good, meseems,[157] as any knight
Toward thy sister's freeing.'

'Ay, Sir Knave!
Ay, knave, because thou strikest as a knight,
995 Being but knave, I hate thee all the more.'

'Fair damsel, you should worship[158] me the more,
That, being but knave, I throw thine enemies.'

'Ay, ay,' she said, 'but thou shalt meet thy match.'

[156] See lines 618-9. The Morning-Star, Noon-Sun, and Evening-Star were the three knights who called themselves the Day. She refers to this as a "fool's parable."
[157] It seems to me.
[158] Honor.

So when they touch'd the second river-loop,
Huge on a huge red horse, and all in mail   1000
Burnish'd to blinding, shone the Noonday Sun
Beyond a raging shallow. As if the flower,
That blows a globe of after arrowlets,[159]
Ten thousand-fold had grown, flash'd the fierce shield,
All sun; and Gareth's eyes had flying blots   1005
Before them when he turn'd from watching him.
He from beyond the roaring shallow roar'd,
'What doest thou, brother, in my marches[160] here?'
And she athwart the shallow thrill'd again,
'Here is a kitchen-knave from Arthur's hall   1010
Hath overthrown thy brother, and hath his arms.'
'Ugh!' cried the Sun, and vizoring[161] up a red
And cipher face of rounded foolishness,
Push'd horse across the foamings of the ford,
Whom Gareth met midstream: no room was there   1015
For lance or tourney-skill: four strokes they struck
With sword, and these were mighty; the new knight
Had fear he might be shamed; but as the Sun
Heaved up a ponderous arm to strike the fifth,
The hoof of his horse slipt in the stream, the stream   1020
Descended, and the Sun was wash'd away.

Then Gareth laid his lance athwart the ford;
So drew him home; but he that fought no more,
As being all bone-batter'd on the rock,

[159] The dandelion.
[160] Within my boundaries, or on my land.
[161] Closing the front part of the helmet by lowering the visor, or
the part raised when not in combat.

1025 Yielded; and Gareth sent him to the King.
    'Myself when I return will plead for thee.'
    'Lead, and I follow.' Quietly she led.
    'Hath not the good wind, damsel, changed again?'
    'Nay, not a point: nor art thou victor here.
1030 There lies a ridge of slate[162] across the ford;
    His horse thereon stumbled — ay, for I saw it.

    '"O Sun" (not this strong fool whom thou, Sir Knave,
    Hast overthrown thro' mere unhappiness),[163]
    "O Sun, that wakenest all to bliss or pain,
1035 O moon, that layest all to sleep again,
    Shine sweetly: twice my love hath smiled on me."

    'What knowest thou of lovesong or of love?
    Nay, nay, God wot,[164] so thou wert nobly born,
    Thou hast a pleasant presence.   Yea, perchance,—

1040 '"O dewy flowers that open to the sun,
    O dewy flowers that close when day is done,
    Blow sweetly: twice my love hath smiled on me."

    'What knowest thou of flowers, except, belike,
    To garnish meats with? hath not our good King
1045 Who lent me thee, the flower of kitchendom,
    A foolish love for flowers? what stick ye round
    The pasty?[165] wherewithal deck the boar's head?
    Flowers? nay, the boar hath rosemaries and bay.

    [162] Probably shale, or slate rock formation.
    [163] Misfortune on his part.
    [164] God knows.
    [165] A large meat or apple pie.

'"O birds, that warble to the morning sky,
O birds that warble as the day goes by,   1050
Sing sweetly: twice my love hath smiled on me."

'What knowest thou of birds, lark, mavis, merle,[166]
Linnet? what dream ye when they utter forth
May-music growing with the growing light,
Their sweet sun-worship? these be for the snare   1055
(So runs thy fancy), these be for the spit,
Larding and basting. See thou have not now
Larded thy last, except thou turn and fly.
There stands the third fool of their allegory.'

For there beyond a bridge of treble bow,   1060
All in a rose-red from the west, and all
Naked it seem'd, and glowing in the broad
Deep-dimpled current underneath, the knight,
That named himself the Star of Evening, stood.

And Gareth, 'Wherefore waits the madman there   1065
Naked in open dayshine?' 'Nay,' she cried,
'Not naked, only wrapt in harden'd skins[167]
That fit him like his own; and so ye cleave
His armour off him, these will turn the blade.'

Then the third brother shouted o'er the bridge,   1070
'O brother-star, why shine ye here so low?
Thy ward is higher up: but have ye slain
The damsel's champion?' and the damsel cried,

[166] Song-thrush and blackbird.
[167] Lynette warns Gareth that this Knight is so used to fighting,
so hardened by valor, that he will be invulnerable even without armor.

'No star of thine, but shot from Arthur's heaven
1075 With all disaster unto thine and thee!
For both thy younger brethren have gone down
Before this youth; and so wilt thou, Sir Star;
Art thou not old?'

       'Old, damsel, old and hard,
Old, with the might and breath of twenty boys.'
1080 Saith Gareth, 'Old, and over-bold in brag!
But that same strength which threw the Morning Star
Can throw the Evening.'

          Then that other blew
A hard and deadly note upon the horn.
'Approach and arm me!' With slow steps from out
1085 An old storm-beaten, russet, many-stain'd
Pavilion, forth a grizzled damsel came,
And arm'd him in old arms, and brought a helm
With but a drying evergreen for crest,[168]
And gave a shield whereon the Star of Even
1090 Half-tarnish'd and half-bright, his emblem, shone.
But when it glitter'd o'er the saddle-bow,
They madly hurl'd together on the bridge;
And Gareth overthrew him, lighted, drew,
There met him drawn,[169] and overthrew him again;
1095 But up like fire he started: and as oft
As Gareth brought him grovelling on his knees,
So many a time he vaulted up again;
Till Gareth panted hard, and his great heart,

[168] A decoration worn on the upper part of the helmet.
[169] With drawn sword.

Foredooming[170] all his trouble was in vain,
Labour'd within him, for he seem'd as one   1100
That all in later, sadder age begins
To war against ill uses of a life,
But these from all his life arise, and cry,
'Thou hast made us lords, and canst not put us down!'
He half despairs; so Gareth seem'd to strike   1105
Vainly, the damsel clamouring all the while,
'Well done, knave-knight, well stricken, O good knight-
       knave —
O knave, as noble as any of all the knights —
Shame me not, shame me not. I have prophesied —
Strike, thou art worthy of the Table Round —   1110
His arms are old, he trusts the harden'd skin —
Strike — strike — the wind will never change again.'[171]
And Gareth hearing ever stronglier smote,
And hew'd great pieces of his armour off him,
But lash'd in vain against the harden'd skin,   1115
And could not wholly bring him under, more
Than loud Southwesterns,[172] rolling ridge on ridge,
The buoy that rides at sea, and dips and springs
For ever; till at length Sir Gareth's brand
Clash'd his, and brake it utterly to the hilt.   1120
'I have thee now;' but forth that other sprang,
And, all unknightlike, writhed his wiry arms
Around him, till he felt, despite his mail,
Strangled, but straining ev'n his uttermost
Cast, and so hurl'd him headlong o'er the bridge   1125

[170] Forejudging, or deciding in advance.
[171] Gareth has at last won the full confidence of Lynette.
[172] Fierce southwest winds at sea.

Down to the river, sink or swim, and cried,
'Lead, and I follow.'

But the damsel said,
'I lead no longer; ride thou at my side;
Thou art the kingliest of all kitchen-knaves.

1130   "'O trefoil,[173] sparkling on the rainy plain,
O rainbow with three colours after rain,
Shine sweetly: thrice my love hath smiled on me.'"

'Sir,— and, good faith, I fain had added — Knight,
But that I heard thee call thyself a knave,—
1135 Shamed am I that I so rebuked, reviled,
Missaid thee; noble I am; and thought the King
Scorn'd me and mine; and now thy pardon, friend,
For thou hast answer'd courteously,
And wholly bold thou art, and meek withal
1140 As any of Arthur's best, but, being knave,
Hast mazed my wit:[174] I marvel what thou art.'

'Damsel,' he said, 'you be not all to blame,
Saving that you mistrusted our good King
Would handle scorn, or yield you, asking, one
1145 Not fit to cope[175] your quest.   You said your say;
Mine answer was my deed.   Good sooth! I hold
He scarce is knight, yea but half-man, nor meet
To fight for gentle damsel, he, who lets

---

[173] Three-leaved clover.
[174] Amazed me.
[175] Not fit to carry out the quest.

His heart be stirr'd with any foolish heat
At any gentle damsel's waywardness.   1150
Shamed! care not! thy foul sayings fought for me:
And seeing now thy words are fair, methinks
There rides no knight, not Lancelot, his great self,
Hath force to quell me.'

                  Nigh upon that hour
When the lone hern[176] forgets his melancholy,   1155
Lets down his other leg, and stretching, dreams
Of goodly supper in the distant pool,
Then turn'd the noble damsel smiling at him,
And told him of a cavern hard at hand,
Where bread and baken meats and good red wine   1160
Of Southland, which the Lady Lyonors
Had sent her coming champion, waited him.

    Anon they past a narrow comb[177] wherein
Were slabs of rock with figures, knights on horse
Sculptured, and deckt in slowly-waning hues.   1165
'Sir Knave, my knight, a hermit once was here,
Whose holy hand hath fashion'd on the rock
The war of Time against the soul of man.
And yon four fools have suck'd their allegory[178]
From these damp walls, and taken but the form.   1170
Know ye not these?' and Gareth lookt and read —
In letters like to those the vexillary[179]

[176] Heron.
[177] Hillside valley.
[178] Gotten the idea of "The Day."
[179] Legion standard-bearer in Roman Army.

Hath left crag-carven o'er the streaming Gelt[180]—
'PHOSPHORUS,' then 'MERIDIES'— 'HESPERUS'—
1175 'Nox'—'MORS,' beneath five figures, armed men,[181]
Slab after slab, their faces forward all,
And running down the Soul, a Shape that fled
With broken wings, torn raiment and loose hair,
For help and shelter to the hermit's cave.
1180 'Follow the faces, and we find it. Look,
Who comes behind!'

                    For one — delay'd at first
Thro' helping back the dislocated Kay
To Camelot, then by what thereafter chanced,
The damsel's headlong error[182] thro' the wood —
1185 Sir Lancelot, having swum the river-loops —
His blue shield-lions cover'd — softly drew
Behind the twain, and when he saw the star
Gleam, on Sir Gareth's turning to him, cried,
'Stay, felon[183] knight, I avenge me for my friend.'
1190 And Gareth crying prick'd against the cry:
But when they closed — in a moment — at one touch
Of that skill'd spear, the wonder of the world —
Went sliding down so easily, and fell,
That when he found the grass within his hands
1195 He laugh'd; the laughter jarr'd upon Lynette:

[180] A small river in Cumberland.
[181] Phosphorus (fŏs-fō´rŭs) is the morning star; Meridies (mĕ-rĭd´ ĭ-ēz), noonday; Hesperus (hĕs´pēr ŭs), evening star; Nox, night; Mors, death. The Soul is seeking refuge in Religion, the hermit's cave.
[182] Wandering.
[183] Treacherous.

Harshly she ask'd him, 'Shamed and overthrown,
And tumbled back into the kitchen-knave,
Why laugh ye? that ye blew your boast in vain?'
'Nay, noble damsel, but that I, the son
Of old King Lot and good Queen Bellicent,   1200
And victor of the bridges and the ford,
And knight of Arthur, here lie thrown by whom
I know not, all thro' mere unhappiness[184]—
Device and sorcery and unhappiness —
Out, sword; we are thrown!' And Lancelot answer'd
          'Prince,   1205
O Gareth — thro' the mere unhappiness
Of one who came to help thee, not to harm,
Lancelot, and all as glad to find thee whole,
As on the day when Arthur knighted him.'

    Then Gareth, 'Thou — Lancelot!— thine the hand 1210
That threw me? And some chance to mar the boast
Thy brethren of thee make — which could not chance—
Had sent thee down before a lesser spear,
Shamed had I been, and sad — O Lancelot — thou!'

    Whereat the maiden, petulant, 'Lancelot,   1215
Why came ye not, when call'd? and wherefore now
Come ye, not call'd? I gloried in my knave,
Who being still rebuked, would answer still
Courteous as any knight — but now, if knight,
The marvel dies, and leaves me fool'd and tricked,   1220
And only wondering wherefore play'd upon:[185]

[184] Mischance, or mishap.
[185] Why I was deceived.

And doubtful whether I and mine be scorn'd.
Where should be truth if not in Arthur's hall,
In Arthur's presence? Knight, knave, prince and fool,
1225 I hate thee and for ever.'[186]

And Lancelot said,
'Blessed be thou, Sir Gareth! knight art thou
To the King's best wish. O damsel, be you wise
To call him shamed, who is but overthrown?
Thrown have I been, nor once, but many a time.
1230 Victor from vanquish'd issues at the last,
And overthrower from being overthrown.
With sword we have not striven; and thy good horse
And thou are weary; yet not less I felt
Thy manhood thro' that wearied lance of thine.
1235 Well hast thou done; for all the stream is freed,
And thou hast wreak'd his justice on his foes,
And when reviled, hast answer'd graciously,
And makest merry when overthrown. Prince, Knight,
Hail, Knight and Prince, and of our Table Round!'

1240   And then when turning to Lynette he told
The tale of Gareth, petulantly she said,
'Ay well — ay well — for worse than being fool'd
Of others, is to fool one's self. A cave,
Sir Lancelot, is hard by, with meats and drinks
1245 And forage for the horse, and flint for fire.
But all about it flies a honeysuckle.
Seek, till we find.' And when they sought and found,
Sir Gareth drank and ate, and all his life

[186] Lynette petulantly denounces her deliverer.

'ast into sleep; on whom the maiden gazed.
Sound sleep be thine! sound cause to sleep hast thou   1250
Vake lusty! Seem I not as tender to him
.s any mother? Ay, but such a one
.s all day long hath rated at her child,
.nd vext his day, but blesses him asleep —
iood lord, how sweetly smells the honeysuckle   1255
n the hush'd night, as if the world were one
)f utter peace, and love, and gentleness!
) Lancelot, Lancelot'— and she clapt her hands —
Full merry am I to find my goodly knave
s knight and noble. See now, sworn have I,   1260
.lse yon black felon[187] had not let me pass,
'o bring thee back to do the battle with him.
'hus an thou goest, he will fight thee first;
Vho doubts thee victor? so will my knight-knave
Iiss the full flower of this accomplishment.'   1265

    Said Lancelot, 'Peradventure[188] he, you name,
Iay know my shield. Let Gareth, an he will,
'hange his for mine, and take my charger, fresh,
'ot to be spurr'd, loving the battle as well
.s he that rides him.' 'Lancelot-like,' she said,   1270
Courteous in this, Lord Lancelot, as in all.'

    And Gareth, wakening, fiercely clutch'd the shield;
Ramp[189] ye lance-splintering lions, on whom all spears
re rotten sticks! ye seem agape to roar!

[187] Wicked knight.
[188] By chance.
[189] Rear on hind legs.

1275 Yea, ramp and roar at leaving of your lord!—
Care not, good beasts, so well I care for you.
O noble Lancelot, from my hold on these
Streams virtue — fire — thro' one that will not shame
Even the shadow of Lancelot under shield.
1280 Hence: let us go.'

             Silent the silent field
They traversed. Arthur's harp[190] tho' summer-wan,
In counter motion to the clouds, allured
The glance of Gareth dreaming on his liege.
A star shot:[191] 'Lo,' said Gareth, 'the foe falls!'
1285 An owl whoopt: 'Hark the victor pealing there!'
Suddenly she that rode upon his left
Clung to the shield that Lancelot lent him, crying,
'Yield, yield him this again: 'tis he must fight:
I curse the tongue that all thro' yesterday
1290 Reviled thee, and hath wrought on Lancelot now
To lend thee horse and shield: wonders ye have done;
Miracles ye cannot: here is glory enow
In having flung the three: I see thee maim'd,
Mangled: I swear thou canst not fling the fourth.'

1295   'And wherefore, damsel? tell me all ye know.
You cannot scare me; nor rough face, or voice,
Brute bulk of limb, or boundless savagery
Appall me from the quest.'

               'Nay, Prince,' she cried
God wot, I never look'd upon the face,

---

[190] The name of a constellation.
[191] Fell.

Seeing he never rides abroad by day;   1300
But watch'd him have I like a phantom pass
Chilling the night: nor have I heard the voice.
Always he made his mouthpiece of a page
Who came and went, and still reported him
As closing in himself the strength of ten,   1305
And when his anger tare him, massacring
Man, woman, lad and girl — yea, the soft babe!
Some hold that he hath swallow'd infant flesh,
Monster! O Prince, I went for Lancelot first,
The quest is Lancelot's: give him back the shield.'   1310

  Said Gareth laughing, 'An he fight for this,
Belike[192] he wins it as the better man:
Thus — and not else!'

              But Lancelot on him urged
All the devisings[193] of their chivalry
When one might meet a mightier than himself;   1315
How best to manage horse, lance, sword and shield,
And so fill up the gap where force might fail
With skill and fineness. Instant[194] were his words.

  Then Gareth, 'Here be rules. I know but one —
To dash against mine enemy and to win.   1320
Yet have I watch'd thee victor in the joust,
And seen thy way.' 'Heaven help thee,' sigh'd Lynette.

[192] Perhaps, probably.
[193] Rules and practices.
[194] Urgent.

Then for a space, and under cloud that grew
To thunder-gloom palling[195] all stars, they rode
1325 In converse till she made her palfrey[196] halt,
Lifted an arm, and softly whisper'd, 'There.'
And all the three were silent seeing, pitch'd
Beside the Castle Perilous on flat field,
A huge pavilion like a mountain peak
1330 Sunder the glooming crimson on the marge,
Black, with black banner, and a long black horn
Beside it hanging; which Sir Gareth graspt,
And so, before the two could hinder him,
Sent all his heart and breath thro' all the horn.
1335 Echo'd the walls; a light twinkled; anon
Came lights and lights, and once again he blew;
Whereon were hollow tramplings up and down
And muffled voices heard, and shadows past;
Till high above him, circled with her maids,
1340 The Lady Lyonors at a window stood,
Beautiful among lights, and waving to him
White hands, and courtesy; but when the Prince
Three times had blown — after long hush — at last –
The huge pavilion slowly yielded up,
1345 Thro' those black foldings, that which housed therein.
High on a nightblack horse, in nightblack arms,
With white breast-bone, and barren ribs of Death,
And crown'd with fleshless laughter[197]—some ten steps–
In the half-light — thro' the dim dawn — advanced
1350 The monster, and then paused, and spake no word.

[195] Darkening, covering as with a pall.
[196] Horse.
[197] A grinning skull.

But Gareth spake and all indignantly,
Fool, for thou hast, men say, the strength of ten,
Canst thou not trust the limbs thy God hath given,
But must, to make the terror of thee more,
Trick thyself out in ghastly imageries   1355
Of that which Life hath done with, and the clod,
Less dull than thou, will hide with mantling flowers
As if for pity?' But he spake no word;
Which set the horror higher: a maiden swoon'd;
The Lady Lyonors wrung her hands and wept,   1360
As doom'd to be the bride of Night and Death;
Sir Gareth's head prickled beneath his helm;
And ev'n Sir Lancelot thro' his warm blood felt
Ice strike, and all that mark'd[198] him were aghast.

At once Sir Lancelot's charger fiercely neigh'd,   1365
And Death's dark war-horse bounded forward with him.
Then those that did not blink[199] the terror, saw
That Death was cast to ground, and slowly rose.
But with one stroke Sir Gareth split the skull.
Half fell to right and half to left and lay.   1370
Then with a stronger buffet he clove the helm
As throughly as the skull; and out from this
Issued the bright face of a blooming boy
Fresh as a flower new-born, and crying, 'Knight,
Slay me not: my three brethren bade me do it,   1375
To make a horror all about the house,
And stay the world from Lady Lyonors.
They never dream'd the passes would be past.'

[198] Noticed him closely.
[199] Shut their eyes so as not to see.

Answer'd Sir Gareth graciously to one
1380 Not many a moon[200] his younger, 'My fair child,
What madness made thee challenge the chief knight
Of Arthur's hall?' 'Fair Sir, they bade me do it.
They hate the King, and Lancelot, the King's friend,
They hoped to slay him somewhere on the stream,
1385 They never dream'd the passes could be past.'

Then sprang the happier day from underground;
And Lady Lyonors and her house, with dance
And revel and song, made merry over Death,
As being after all their foolish fears
1390 And horrors only proven a blooming boy.
So large mirth lived and Gareth won the quest.

And he[201] that told the tale in older times
Says that Sir Gareth wedded Lyonors,
But he,[202] that told it later, says Lynette.

[206] Not many months.
[201] Malory.
[202] Tennyson.

LANCELOT AND ELAINE

ELAINE[1] the fair, Elaine the lovable,
Elaine, the lily maid of Astolat,[2]
High in her chamber up a tower to the east
Guarded the sacred shield of Lancelot;
Which first she placed where morning's earliest ray   5
Might strike it, and awake her with the gleam;
Then fearing rust or soilure fashion'd for it
A case of silk, and braided thereupon
All the devices[3] blazon'd on the shield
In their own tinct,[4] and added, of her wit,[5]   10
A border fantasy of branch and flower,
And yellow-throated nestling in the nest.
Nor rested thus content, but day by day,
Leaving her household and good father, climb'd
That eastern tower, and entering barr'd her door,   15
Stript off the case, and read the naked shield,
Now guess'd a hidden meaning in his arms,
Now made a pretty history to herself
Of every dint a sword had beaten in it,
And every scratch a lance had made upon it,   20
Conjecturing when and where: this cut is fresh;
That ten years back; this dealt him at Caerlyle;[6]

[1] Elaine (ĕ-lān'). The Celtic name for Helen.
[2] Closely identified with Guildford, in Surrey.
[3] The emblems carved on the shield.
[4] Each in its own color.
[5] Out of her fancy, or imagination.
[6] The location of a famous combat.

That at Caerleon;[7] this at Camelot:[8]
And ah God's mercy, what a stroke was there!
25 And here a thrust that might have kill'd, but God
Broke the strong lance, and roll'd his enemy down,
And saved him: so she lived in fantasy.

How came the lily maid by that good shield
Of Lancelot, she that knew not ev'n his name?
30 He left it with her, when he rode to tilt
For the great diamond in the diamond jousts,
Which Arthur had ordain'd, and by that name
Had named them, since a diamond was the prize.

For Arthur, long before they crown'd him King,
35 Roving the trackless realms of Lyonesse,[9]
Had found a glen, gray boulder and black tarn.
A horror lived about the tarn, and clave
Like its own mists to all the mountain side:
For here two brothers, one a king, had met
40 And fought together; but their names were lost;
And each had slain his brother at a blow;
And down they fell and made the glen abhorr'd:
And there they lay till all their bones were bleach'd,
And lichen'd[10] into colour with the crags:
45 And he, that once was king, had on a crown
Of diamonds, one in front, and four aside.[11]

---

[7] Caerleon was represented as one of Arthur's capitals.
[8] The capital of Arthur.
[9] The country where Arthur grew up.
[10] Covered with lichens to look like the surrounding rocks.
[11] Four on each side.

And Arthur came, and labouring up the pass,
All in a misty moonshine, unawares
Had trodden that crown'd skeleton, and the skull
Brake from the nape,[12] and from the skull the crown   50
Roll'd into light, and turning on its rims
Fled like a glittering rivulet to the tarn:
And down the shingly scaur[13] he plunged, and caught,
And set it on his head, and in his heart
Heard murmurs, 'Lo, thou likewise shalt be King.'   55

    Thereafter, when a King, he had the gems
Pluck'd from the crown, and show'd them to his knights
Saying, 'These jewels, whereupon I chanced
Divinely,[14] are the kingdom's, not the King's —
For public use: henceforward let there be,   60
Once every year, a joust for one of these:
For so by nine years' proof we needs must learn
Which is our mightiest, and ourselves shall grow
In use of arms and manhood, till we drive
The heathen, who, some say, shall rule the land   65
Hereafter, which God hinder.' Thus he spoke:
And eight years past, eight jousts had been, and still
Had Lancelot won the diamond of the year,
With purpose to present them to the Queen,
When all were won; but meaning all at once   70
To snare her royal fancy with a boon
Worth half her realm, had never spoken word.

[12] The upper neck.
[13] The steep rocky cliff.
[14] By divine help.

Now for the central diamond and the last
And largest, Arthur, holding then his court
75 Hard on the river nigh the place which now
Is this world's hugest,[15] let proclaim a joust
At Camelot, and when the time drew nigh
Spake (for she had been sick) to Guinevere,
'Are you so sick, my Queen, you cannot move
80 To these fair jousts?' 'Yea, lord,' she said, 'ye know
          it.'
'Then will ye miss,' he answer'd, 'the great deeds
Of Lancelot, and his prowess in the lists,
A sight ye love to look on.' And the Queen
Lifted her eyes, and they dwelt languidly
85 On Lancelot, where he stood beside the King.
He thinking that he read her meaning there,
'Stay with me, I am sick; my love is more
Than many diamonds,' yielded; and a heart
Love-loyal to the least wish of the Queen
90 (However much he yearn'd to make complete
The tale[16] of diamonds for his destined boon)
Urged him to speak against the truth, and say,
'Sir King, mine ancient wound is hardly whole,
And lets[17] me from the saddle;' and the King
95 Glanced first at him, then her, and went his way.
No sooner gone than suddenly she began:

'To blame, my lord Sir Lancelot, much to blame!
Why go ye not to these fair jousts? the knights

---

[15] The City of London.
[16] The complete number.
[17] Hinders me from riding.

Are half of them our enemies, and the crowd
Will murmur, "Lo, the shameless ones, who take   100
Their pastime now the trustful King is gone!'"
Then Lancelot vext at having lied in vain:
'Are ye so wise? ye were not once so wise,
My Queen, that summer, when ye loved me first.
Then of the crowd ye took no more account   105
Than of the myriad cricket of the mead,
When its own voice clings to each blade of grass,
And every voice is nothing. As to knights,
Them surely can I silence with all ease.
But now my loyal worship is allow'd[18]   110
Of all men: many a bard, without offence,
Has link'd our names together in his lay.
Lancelot, the flower of bravery, Guinevere,
The pearl of beauty: and our knights at feast
Have pledged us in this union, while the King   115
Would listen smiling. How then? is there more?
Has Arthur spoken aught? or would yourself,
Now weary of my service and devoir,[19]
Henceforth be truer to your faultless lord?'

    She broke into a little scornful laugh: 120
'Arthur, my lord, Arthur, the faultless King,
That passionate perfection, my good lord —
But who can gaze upon the Sun in heaven?
He never spake word of reproach to me,
He never had a glimpse of mine untruth,   125
He cares not for me: only here to-day

[18] Admitted and understood.
[19] Service and dutiful attentions.

There gleam'd a vague suspicion in his eyes:[20]
Some meddling rogue has tamper'd with him — else
Rapt in this fancy of his Table Round,
130 And swearing men to vows impossible,
To make them like himself: but, friend, to me
He is all fault who hath no fault at all:
For who loves me must have a touch of earth;
The low sun makes the colour: I am yours,
135 Not Arthur's, as ye know, save by the bond.
And therefore hear my words: go to the jousts:
The tiny-trumpeting gnat can break our dream
When sweetest,[21] and the vermin voices here
May buzz so loud — we scorn them, but they sting.'

140   Then answer'd Lancelot, the chief of knights:
'And with what face, after my pretext made,
Shall I appear, O Queen, at Camelot, I
Before a King who honours his own word,
As if it were his God's?'

                              'Yea,' said the Queen,
145 'A moral child without the craft to rule,[22]
Else had he not lost me: but listen to me,
If I must find you wit: we hear it said
That men go down before your spear at a touch,
But knowing you are Lancelot; your great name,
150 This conquers: hide it therefore; go unknown:
Win! by this kiss you will: and our true King

    [20] See line 95.
    [21] So the least bit of gossip can mar our happiness.
    [22] Good, without the skill to govern.

Will then allow your pretext, O my knight,
As all for glory; for to speak him true,
Ye know right well, how meek soe'er he seem,
No keener hunter after glory breathes.   155
He loves it in his knights more than himself:
They prove to him his work: win and return.'

      Then got Sir Lancelot suddenly to horse,
Wroth at himself. Not willing to be known,
He left the barren-beaten thoroughfare,   160
Chose the green path that show'd the rarer foot,
And there among the solitary downs,[23]
Full often lost in fancy, lost his way;
Till as he traced a faintly-shadow'd track,
That all in loops and links among the dales   165
Ran to the Castle of Astolat, he saw
Fired from the west,[24] far on a hill, the towers.
Thither he made, and blew the gateway horn.
Then came an old, dumb, myriad-wrinkled man,
Who let him into lodging and disarm'd.   170
And Lancelot marvell'd at the wordless man;
And issuing found the Lord of Astolat
With two strong sons, Sir Torre and Sir Lavaine,
Moving to meet him in the castle court;
And close behind them stept the lily maid   175
Elaine, his daughter: mother of the house
There was not: some light jest among them rose
With laughter dying down as the great knight
Approach'd them: then the Lord of Astolat:

[23] Lonely bare hills used for grazing.
[24] With windows reflecting the setting sun.

180 'Whence comest thou, my guest, and by what name
     Livest between the lips? for by thy state
     And presence I might guess thee chief of those,
     After the King, who eat in Arthur's halls.
     Him have I seen: the rest, his Table Round,
185 Known as they are, to me they are unknown.'

     Then answer'd Lancelot, the chief of knights:
     'Known am I, and of Arthur's hall, and known,
     What I by mere mischance have brought, my shield.
     But since I go to joust as one unknown
190 At Camelot for the diamond, ask me not,
     Hereafter ye shall know me — and the shield —
     I pray you lend me one, if such you have,
     Blank, or at least with some device not mine.'

     Then said the Lord of Astolat, 'Here is Torre's:
195 Hurt in his first tilt was my son, Sir Torre.
     And so, God wot, his shield is blank enough.
     His ye can have.' Then added plain Sir Torre,
     'Yea, since I cannot use it, ye may have it.'
     Here laugh'd the father saying, 'Fie, Sir Churl,
200 Is that an answer for a noble knight?
     Allow him!25 but Lavaine, my younger here,
     He is so full of lustihood,26 he will ride,
     Joust for it, and win, and bring it in an hour,
     And set it in this damsel's golden hair,
205 To make her thrice as wilful as before.'

     25 Pardon him.
     26 Courage and enthusiasm.

'Nay, father, nay, good father, shame me not
Before this noble knight,' said young Lavaine,
'For nothing. Surely I but play'd on Torre:
He seemed so sullen, vext he could not go:
A jest, no more! for knight, the maiden dreamt   210
That some one put this diamond in her hand,
And that it was too slippery to be held,
And slipt and fell into some pool or stream,
The castle-well, belike; and then I said
That *if* I went, and *if* I fought and won it   215
(But all was jest and joke among ourselves)
Then must she keep it safelier. All was jest.
But, father, give me leave, an if he will,
To ride to Camelot with this noble knight:
Win shall I not, but do my best to win: 220
Young as I am, yet would I do my best.'

'So ye will grace[27] me,' answer'd Lancelot,
Smiling a moment, 'with your fellowship
O'er these waste downs whereon I lost myself,
Then were I glad of you as guide and friend: 225
And you shall win this diamond, — as I hear
It is a fair large diamond, — if ye may,
And yield[28] it to this maiden, if ye will.'
'A fair large diamond,' added plain Sir Torre,
'Such be for queens, and not for simple maids.'   230
Then she, who held her eyes upon the ground,
Elaine, and heard her name so tost about,
Flush'd slightly at the slight disparagement

27 Favor.
28 Give.

Before the stranger knight, who, looking at her,
235 Full courtly, yet not falsely, thus return'd:
  'If what is fair be but for what is fair,
  And only queens are to be counted so,
  Rash were my judgment then, who deem this maid
  Might wear as fair a jewel as is on earth,
240 Not violating the bond of like to like.'

  He spoke and ceased: the lily maid Elaine,
  Won by the mellow voice before she look'd,
  Lifted her eyes, and read his lineaments.
  The great and guilty love he bare the Queen,
245 In battle with the love he bare his lord,
  Had marr'd his face and mark'd it ere his time.
  Another sinning on such heights with one,
  The flower of all the west and all the world,
  Had been the sleeker for it: but in him
250 His mood was often like a fiend, and rose
  And drove him into wastes and solitudes
  For agony, who was yet a living soul.
  Marr'd as he was, he seem'd the goodliest man
  That ever among ladies ate in hall,
255 And noblest, when she lifted up her eyes.
  However marr'd, of more than twice her years,
  Seam'd with an ancient swordcut on the cheek,
  And bruised and bronzed, she lifted up her eyes
  And loved him, with that love which was her doom.

260   Then the great knight, the darling of the court,
  Loved of the loveliest, into that rude hall
  Stept with all grace, and not with half disdain

Hid under grace, as in a smaller time,
But kindly man moving among his kind:
Whom they with meats and vintage of their best 265
And talk and minstrel melody entertain'd.
And much they ask'd of court and Table Round,
And ever well and readily answer'd he:
But Lancelot, when they glanced at Guinevere,
Suddenly speaking of the wordless man, 270
Heard from the Baron that, ten years before,
The heathen caught and reft him of his tongue.[29]
'He learnt and warn'd me of their fierce design
Against my house, and him they caught and maim'd;
But I, my sons and little daughter fled 275
From bonds or death, and dwelt among the woods
By the great river in a boatman's hut.
Dull days were those, till our good Arthur broke
The Pagan yet once more on Badon hill.'[30]

'O there, great lord, doubtless,' Lavaine said, rapt[31] 280
By all the sweet and sudden passion of youth
Toward greatness in its elder, 'you have fought.
O tell us — for we live apart — you know
Of Arthur's glorious wars.' And Lancelot spoke
And answer'd him at full, as having been 285
With Arthur in the fight which all day long
Rang by the white mouth of the violent Glem;[32]
And in the four loud battles by the shore

[29] Tore out his tongue.
[30] Badon hill was the scene of one of Arthur's great battles.
[31] Carried away.
[32] Here begins the account of Arthur's twelve most famous battles.

Of Duglas; that on Bassa; then the war
290 That thunder'd in and out the gloomy skirts
Of Celidon the forest; and again
By castle Gurnion, where the glorious King
Had on his cuirass[33] worn our Lady's Head,[34]
Carv'd of one emerald centr'd in a sun
295 Of silver rays, that lighten'd as he breathed;
And at Caerleon had he help'd his lord,
When the strong neighings of the wild white Horse[35]
Set every gilded parapet[36] shuddering;
And up in Agned-Cathregonion too,
300 And down the waste sand-shores of Trath Treroit,
Where many a heathen fell; 'and on the mount
Of Badon I myself beheld the King
Charge at the head of all his Table Round,
And all his legions crying Christ and him,[37]
305 And break them; and I saw him, after, stand
High on a heap of slain, from spur to plume
Red as the rising sun with heathen blood,
And seeing me, with a great voice he cried,
"They are broken, they are broken!" for the King,
310 However mild he seems at home, nor cares
For triumph in our mimic wars, the jousts —
For if his own knight cast him down, he laughs
Saying, his knights are better men than he —

[33] Breastplate, originally of leather, later of metal.
[34] The image of the head of the Virgin Mary.
[35] A white horse was the national emblem of the Saxons.
[36] A breastwork or fortification on top of the main defense wall.
[37] The war-cry of the Arthurian warriors was "Christ and King Arthur!"

Yet in this heathen war the fire of God
Fills him: I never saw his like: there lives   315
No greater leader.'

                    While he utter'd this,
Low to her own heart said the lily maid,
'Save your great self, fair lord;' and when he fell
From talk of war to traits of pleasantry —
Being mirthful he, but in a stately kind —   320
She still took note that when the living smile
Died from his lips, across him came a cloud
Of melancholy severe, from which again,
Whenever in her hovering to and fro
The lily maid had striven to make him cheer,   325
There brake a sudden-beaming tenderness
Of manners and of nature: and she thought
That all was nature, all, perchance, for her.
And all night long his face before her lived,
As when a painter, poring on a face,   330
Divinely thro' all hindrance finds the man
Behind it, and so paints him that his face,
The shape and colour of a mind and life,
Lives for his children, ever at its best
And fullest; so the face before her lived,   335
Dark-splendid, speaking in the silence, full
Of noble things, and held her from her sleep.
Till rathe[38] she rose, half-cheated in the thought
She needs must bid farewell to sweet Lavaine.
First as in fear, step after step, she stole   340
Down the long tower-stairs, hesitating:

[38] Very early.

Anon,[39] she heard Sir Lancelot cry in the court,
'This shield, my friend, where is it?' and Lavaine
Past inward, as she came from out the tower.
345 There to his proud horse Lancelot turn'd, and smooth'd
The glossy shoulder, humming to himself.
Half-envious of the flattering hand, she drew
Nearer and stood. He look'd, and more amazed
Than if seven men had set upon him, saw
350 The maiden standing in the dewy light.
He had not dream'd she was so beautiful.
Then came on him a sort of sacred fear,
For silent, tho' he greeted her, she stood
Rapt on his face as if it were a God's.
355 Suddenly flash'd on her a wild desire,
That he should wear her favour at the tilt.
She braved a riotous[40] heart in asking for it.
'Fair lord, whose name I know not — noble it is,
I well believe, the noblest — will you wear
360 My favour[41] at this tourney?' 'Nay,' said he,
'Fair lady, since I never yet have worn
Favour of any lady in the lists.[42]
Such is my wont, as those, who know me, know.'
'Yea, so,' she answer'd; 'then in wearing mine
365 Needs must be lesser likelihood, noble lord,
That those who know should know you.' And he turn'd
Her counsel up and down within his mind,

[39] Straightway, soon.
[40] She asked in spite of her fast-beating heart.
[41] It was customary for the knight to wear some lady's token, c
favor, when on his quest or when in tilt or tournament.
[42] The inclosure around the tournament field.

nd found it true, and answer'd, 'True, my child.
Vell, I will wear it: fetch it out to me:
Vhat is it?' and she told him 'A red sleeve   370
sroider'd with pearls,' and brought it: then he bound
Ier token on his helmet, with a smile
aying, 'I never yet have done so much
'or any maiden living,' and the blood
prang to her face and fill'd her with delight;   375
sut left her all the paler, when Lavaine
teturning brought the yet-unblazon'd shield,
Iis brother's; which he gave to Lancelot,
Vho parted with his own to fair Elaine:
Do me this grace, my child, to have my shield   380
n keeping till I come.' 'A grace to me,'
he answer'd, 'twice to-day. I am your squire!'
Vhereat Lavaine said, laughing, 'Lily maid,
'or fear our people call you lily maid
n earnest, let me bring your colour back;   385
)nce, twice, and thrice: now get you hence to bed:'
o kiss'd her, and Sir Lancelot his own hand,
nd thus they moved away: she stay'd a minute,
'hen made a sudden step to the gate, and there —
Ier bright hair blown about the serious face   390
'et rosy-kindled with her brother's kiss —
'aused by the gateway, standing near the shield
n silence, while she watch'd their arms far-off
parkle, until they dipt below the downs.
'hen to her tower she climb'd, and took the shield,   395
'here kept it, and so lived in fantasy.[43]

[43] Imagination or fancy.

Meanwhile the new companions past away
Far o'er the long backs of the bushless downs,
To where Sir Lancelot knew there lived a knight
400 Not far from Camelot, now for forty years
A hermit, who had pray'd, labour'd and pray'd,
And ever labouring had scoop'd himself
In the white rock a chapel and a hall
On massive columns, like a shorecliff cave,
405 And cells and chambers: all were fair and dry;
The green light from the meadows underneath
Struck up and lived along the milky roofs;
And in the meadows tremulous aspen-trees
And poplars made a noise of falling showers.
410 And thither wending there that night they bode.

But when the next day broke from underground,[44]
And shot red fire and shadows thro' the cave,
They rose, heard mass, broke fast, and rode away:
Then Lancelot saying, 'Hear, but hold my name
415 Hidden, you ride with Lancelot of the Lake,'
Abash'd Lavaine, whose instant reverence,
Dearer to true young hearts than their own praise,
But left him leave to stammer, 'Is it indeed?'
And after muttering 'The great Lancelot,'
420 At last he got his breath and answer'd, 'One,
One have I seen — that other, our liege lord,
The dread Pendragon,[45] Britain's King of kings,

[44] The ancient Greeks thought the sun rose from an underworld
Tennyson embodies their idea here.

[45] Meaning *head-ruler*. A title given to Britain's most renowned
kings — first to Uther, father of Arthur.

f whom the people talk mysteriously,
e will be there — then were I stricken blind
hat minute, I might say that I had seen.'   425

 So spake Lavaine, and when they reach'd the lists
y Camelot in the meadow, let his eyes
un thro' the peopled[46] gallery which half round
ay like a rainbow fall'n upon the grass,
ntil they found the clear-faced King, who sat   430
obed in red samite,[47] easily to be known,
nce to his crown the golden dragon clung,
nd down his robe the dragon writhed in gold,
nd from the carven-work behind him crept
wo dragons gilded, sloping down to make   435
rms for his chair, while all the rest of them
hro' knots and loops and folds innumerable
ed ever thro' the woodwork, till they found
he new design wherein they lost themselves,
et with all ease, so tender was the work: 440
nd, in the costly canopy o'er him set,
lazed the last diamond of the nameless king.

 Then Lancelot answer'd young Lavaine and said
Ie you call great: mine is the firmer seat,
he truer lance: but there is many a youth   445
ow crescent,[48] who will come to all I am
nd overcome it; and in me there dwells
o greatness, save it be some far-off touch

[46] The crowded seating-space.
[47] A heavy rich silk used for royal robes.
[48] Now developing into knighthood.

Of greatness to know well I am not great:
450 There is the man.' And Lavaine gaped[49] upon him
As on a thing miraculous, and anon
The trumpets blew; and then did either side,
They that assail'd, and they that held the lists,[50]
Set lance in rest,[51] strike spur, suddenly move,
455 Meet in the midst, and there so furiously
Shock, that a man far-off might well perceive,
If any man that day were left afield,[52]
The hard earth shake, and a low thunder of arms.
And Lancelot bode[53] a little, till he saw
460 Which were the weaker; then he hurl'd into it
Against the stronger: little need to speak
Of Lancelot in his glory! King, duke, earl,
Count. baron — whom he smote, he overthrew.

But in the field were Lancelot's kith and kin,[54]
465 Ranged with the Table Round that held the lists,
Strong men, and wrathful that a stranger knight
Should do and almost overdo the deeds
Of Lancelot; and one said to the other, 'Lo!
What[55] is he? I do not mean the force alone —
470 The grace and versatility of the man!
Is it not Lancelot?' 'When has Lancelot worn

[49] Stared with wide open mouth.

[50] One party defended the field, or held the lists, against the atta
of the other.

[51] A support for the lance in fighting.

[52] In his field at home.

[53] Waited to see which side most needed help.

[54] Friends and relatives.

[55] Who.

'avour of any lady in the lists?
[ot such his wont, as we, that know him, know.'
How then? who then?' a fury seized them all,
. fiery family passion for the name   475
)f Lancelot, and a glory one with theirs.
'hey couch'd[56] their spears and prick'd[57] their steeds,
          and thus,
'heir plumes driv'n backward by the wind they made
n moving, all together down upon him
3are, as a wild wave in the wide North-sea,   480
rreen-glimmering toward the summit, bears, with all
ts stormy crests that smoke against the skies,
)own on a bark, and overbears the bark,
.nd him that helms[58] it, so they overbore
ir Lancelot and his charger, and a spear   485
)own-glancing lamed the charger, and a spear
*rick'd sharply his own cuirass, and the head
*ierced thro' his side, and there snapt, and remain'd.

   Then Sir Lavaine did well and worshipfully;[59]
Ie bore a knight of old repute to the earth,   490
.nd brought his horse to Lancelot where he lay.
Ie up the side, sweating with agony, got,
3ut thought to do while he might yet endure,[60]
.nd being lustily holpen[61] by the rest,

----

[56] Lowered their spears for the attack.
[57] Spurred.
[58] Steers it.
[59] Honorably.
[60] Fight while he had strength.
[61] Helped.

495 His party,[62]— tho' it seem'd half-miracle
    To those he fought with, — drave his kith and kin,
    And all the Table Round that held the lists,
    Back to the barrier; then the trumpets blew
    Proclaiming his the prize, who wore the sleeve
500 Of scarlet, and the pearls; and all the knights,
    His party, cried, 'Advance and take thy prize
    The diamond;' but he answer'd, 'Diamond me
    No diamonds![63] for God's love, a little air!
    Prize me no prizes, for my prize is death!
505 Hence will I, and I charge you, follow me not.'

    He spoke, and vanish'd suddenly from the field
    With young Lavaine into the poplar grove.
    There from his charger[64] down he slid, and sat,
    Gasping to Sir Lavaine, 'Draw the lance-head:'
510 'Ah my sweet lord Sir Lancelot,' said Lavaine,
    'I dread me, if I draw it, you will die.'
    But he, 'I die already with it: draw —
    Draw,'— and Lavaine drew, and Sir Lancelot gave
    A marvellous great shriek and ghastly groan,
515 And half his blood burst forth, and down he sank
    For the pure pain,[65] and wholly swoon'd away.
    Then came the hermit out and bare him in,
    There stanch'd his wound; and there, in daily doubt
    Whether to live or die, for many a week

    [62] Lancelot had joined the side fighting against the Round Tabl
    knights.
    [63] Talk not to me of diamonds.
    [64] War-horse.
    [65] From sheer pain.

id from the wide world's rumour by the grove   520
f poplars with their noise of falling showers,
nd ever-tremulous aspen-trees, he lay.

But on that day when Lancelot fled the lists,
is party, knights of utmost North and West,
ords of waste marches, kings of desolate isles,   525
ame round their great Pendragon, saying to him,
Lo, Sire, our knight, thro' whom we won the day,
ath gone sore wounded, and hath left his prize
ntaken, crying that his prize is death.'
Heaven hinder,' said the King, 'that such an one,   530
o great a knight as we have seen to-day —
e seem'd to me another Lancelot —
ea, twenty times I thought him Lancelot —
e must not pass uncared for. Wherefore, rise,
Gawain, and ride forth and find the knight.   535
Wounded and wearied needs must he be near.
charge you that you get at once to horse.
nd, knights and kings, there breathes not one of you
Will deem this prize of ours is rashly given:
lis prowess[66] was too wondrous. We will do him   540
To customary honour: since the knight
ame not to us, of us to claim the prize,
urselves will send it after. Rise and take
his diamond, and deliver it, and return,
nd bring us[67] where he is, and how he fares,   545
nd cease not from your quest until ye find.'

[66] Courage and skill.
[67] Bring us news of where he is, etc.

So saying, from the carven flower above,
To which it made a restless heart, he took,
And gave, the diamond: then from where he sat,
550 At Arthur's right, with smiling face arose,
. With smiling face and frowning heart, a Prince
In the mid might and flourish of his May,[68]
Gawain, surnamed The Courteous, fair and strong,
And after Lancelot, Tristram, and Geraint,
555 And Gareth, a good knight, but therewithal
Sir Modred's brother, and the child of Lot,
Nor often loyal to his word, and now
Wroth that the King's command to sally forth
In quest of whom he knew not, made him leave
560 The banquet, and concourse of knights and kings.

So all in wrath he got to horse and went;
While Arthur to the banquet, dark in mood,
Past, thinking, 'Is it Lancelot who hath come
Despite the wound he spake of, all for gain
565 Of glory, and hath added wound to wound,
And ridd'n away to die?' So fear'd the King,
And, after two days' tarriance[69] there, return'd.
Then when he saw the Queen, embracing ask'd,
'Love, are you yet so sick?' 'Nay, lord,' she said.
570 'And where is Lancelot?' Then the Queen amazed,
'Was he not with you? won he not your prize?'
'Nay, but one like him.' 'Why that like was he.'
And when the King demanded how she knew,
Said, 'Lord, no sooner had ye parted from us,

[68] Youthful prime.
[69] Sojourn, or stay.

han Lancelot told me of a common talk[70]   575
hat men went down before his spear at a touch,
ut knowing he was Lancelot; his great name
onquer'd; and therefore would he hide his name
rom all men, ev'n the King, and to this end
ad made the pretext of a hindering wound,   580
hat he might joust unknown of all, and learn
his old prowess were in aught decay'd;
nd added, "Our true Arthur, when he learns,
ill well allow my pretext, as for gain
f purer glory."'

                Then replied the King: —   585
ar lovelier in our Lancelot had it been,
a lieu of idly dallying with the truth,
o have trusted me as he hath trusted thee.
urely his King and most familiar friend
ight well have kept his secret. True, indeed,   590
lbeit[71] I know my knights fantastical,[72]
o fine[73] a fear in our large Lancelot
ust needs have moved my laughter: now remains
ut little cause for laughter: his own kin —
l news, my Queen, for all who love him, this! —   595
is kith and kin, not knowing, set upon him;
o that he went sore wounded from the field:
et good news too: for goodly hopes are mine
hat Lancelot is no more a lonely heart.

[70] The queen had suggested this (l. 147 ff).
[71] Although.
[72] Full of passing whims and fancies.
[73] So refined a fear, or a fear born of over-sensitiveness.

600 He wore, against his wont, upon his helm
A sleeve of scarlet, broider'd with great pearls,
Some gentle maiden's gift.'

                              'Yea, lord,' she said,
'Thy hopes are mine,' and saying that, she choked,
And sharply turn'd about to hide her face,
605 Past to her chamber, and there flung herself
Down on the great King's couch, and writhed upon i
And clench'd her fingers till they bit the palm,
And shriek'd out 'Traitor' to the unhearing wall,
Then flash'd into wild tears, and rose again,
610 And moved about her palace, proud and pale.

    Gawain the while thro' all the region round
Rode with his diamond, wearied of the quest,
Touch'd at all points, except the poplar grove,
And came at last, tho' late, to Astolat:
615 Whom glittering in enamell'd arms the maid
Glanced at, and cried, 'What news from Camelot, lord
What of the knight with the red sleeve?' 'He won.'
'I knew it,' she said. 'But parted from the jousts
Hurt in the side,' whereat she caught her breath;
620 Thro' her own side she felt the sharp lance go;
Thereon she smote her hand: wellnigh she swoon'd:
And, while he gazed wonderingly at her, came
The Lord of Astolat out, to whom the Prince
Reported who he was, and on what quest
625 Sent, that he bore the prize and could not find
The victor, but had ridd'n a random round[74]

    [74] Had ridden hard hither and thither, at random, or aimlessly.

'o seek him, and had wearied of the search.
'o whom the Lord of Astolat, 'Bide with us,
nd ride no more at random, noble Prince!
Iere was the knight, and here he left a shield;   630
'his will he send or come for: furthermore
Iur son is with him; we shall hear anon,
Ieeds must we hear.' To this the courteous Prince
ccorded with his wonted courtesy,
ourtesy with a touch of traitor in it,   635
nd stay'd; and cast his eyes on fair Elaine:
Vhere could be found face daintier? then her shape
rom forehead down to foot, perfect — again
rom foot to forehead exquisitely turn'd:
Vell — if I bide, lo! this wild flower for me!'   640
nd oft they met among the garden yews,
nd there he set himself to play upon her
Vith sallying wit, free flashes from a height
bove her, graces of the court, and songs,
ighs, and slow smiles, and golden eloquence   645
nd amorous adulation, till the maid
ebell'd against it, saying to him, 'Prince,
 loyal nephew of our noble King,
'hy ask you not to see the shield he left,
'hence you might learn his name? Why slight your
          King,   650
nd lose the quest he sent you on, and prove
'o surer than our falcon yesterday,
Vho lost the hern we slipt her at, and went
o all the winds?'[75] Nay, by mine head,' said he,
 lose it, as we lose the lark in heaven,   655

[75] Went away not to return.

O damsel, in the light of your blue eyes;
But an ye will it let me see the shield.'
And wnen the shield was brought, and Gawain saw
Sir Lancelot's azure lions, crown'd with gold,
660 Ramp in the field, he smote his thigh, and mock'd:
'Right was the King! our Lancelot! that true man!'
'And right was I,' she answer'd merrily, 'I,
Who dream'd my knight the greatest knight of all.'
'And if I dream'd,' said Gawain, 'that you love
665 This greatest knight, your pardon! lo, ye know it!
Speak therefore: shall I waste myself in vain?'
Full simple was her answer, 'What know I?
My brethren have been all my fellowship,[76]
And I, when often they have talk'd of love,
670 Wish'd it had been my mother, for they talk'd,
Meseem'd, of what they knew not; so myself —
I know not if I know what true love is,
But if I know, then, if I love not him,
I know there is none other I can love.'
675 'Yea, by God's death,'[77] said he, 'ye love him well,
But would not, knew ye what all others know,
And whom he loves.' 'So be it,' cried Elaine,
And lifted her fair face and moved away:
But he pursued her, calling, 'Stay a little!
680 One golden minute's grace! he wore your sleeve:
Would he break faith with one I may not name?
Must our true man change like a leaf at last?
Nay — like enow: why then, far be it from me
To cross our mighty Lancelot in his loves!

[76] My brothers have been my only companions.
[77] A common form of oath, by the death on the cross.

nd, damsel, for I deem[78] you know full well   685
Vhere your great knight is hidden, let me leave
Iy quest with you; the diamond also: here!
'or if you love, it will be sweet to give it;
nd if he love, it will be sweet to have it
'rom your own hand; and whether he love or not,   690
. diamond is a diamond. Fare you well
. thousand times! — a thousand times farewell!
'et, if he love, and his love hold, we two
Iay meet at court hereafter: there, I think,
o ye will learn the courtesies of the court,   695
Ve two shall know each other.'

                   Then he gave,
nd slightly kiss'd the hand to which he gave,
'he diamond, and all wearied of the quest
eapt on his horse, and carolling as he went
. true-love ballad, lightly rode away.   700

  Thence to the court he past; there told the King
Vhat the King knew, 'Sir Lancelot is the knight.'
nd added, 'Sir, my liege, so much I learnt;
Sut fail'd to find him, tho' I rode all round
'he region: but I lighted on[79] the maid   705
Vhose sleeve he wore; she loves him; and to her,
)eeming our courtesy is the truest law,
gave the diamond: she will render it;
'or by mine head she knows his hiding-place.'

[78] Judge.
[79] Came by chance to find.

710   The seldom-frowning King frown'd, and replied,
      'Too courteous truly! ye shall go no more
      On quest of mine, seeing that ye forget
      Obedience is the courtesy due to kings.'

      He spake and parted. Wroth, but all in awe,
715 For twenty strokes of the blood,[80] without a word,
      Linger'd that other, staring after him;
      Then shook his hair, strode off, and buzz'd abroad
      About the maid of Astolat, and her love.
      All ears were prick'd at once, all tongues were loosed:
720 'The maid of Astolat loves Sir Lancelot,
      Sir Lancelot loves the maid of Astolat.'
      Some read the King's face, some the Queen's, and all
      Had marvel what the maid might be, but most
      Predoom'd[81] her as unworthy. One old dame
725 Came suddenly on the Queen with the sharp news.
      She, that had heard the noise of it before,
      But sorrowing Lancelot should have stoop'd so low,
      Marr'd her friend's aim with pale tranquillity.[82]
      So ran the tale like fire about the court,
730 Fire in dry stubble a nine-days' wonder flared:
      Till ev'n the knights at banquet twice or thrice
      Forgot to drink to Lancelot and the Queen,
      And pledging[83] Lancelot and the lily maid
      Smiled at each other, while the Queen, who sat
735 With lips severely placid, felt the knot

---

[80] Stood there during twenty heart-beats.
[81] Pre-judged, or decided in advance.
[82] Spoiled the friend's purpose by calmness.
[83] Drinking a health to.

Climb in her throat, and with her feet unseen
Crush'd the wild passion out against the floor
Beneath the banquet, where the meats became
As wormwood,[84] and she hated all who pledged.

But far away the maid in Astolat,   740
Her guiltless rival, she that ever kept
The one-day-seen Sir Lancelot in her heart,
Crept to her father, while he mused alone,
Sat on his knee, stroked his gray face and said,
'Father, you call me wilful, and the fault   745
Is yours who let me have my will, and now,
Sweet father, will you let me lose my wits?'
'Nay,' said he, 'surely.' 'Wherefore, let me hence,'
She answer'd, 'and find out our dear Lavaine.'
'Ye will not lose your wits for dear Lavaine: 751
Bide,' answer'd he: 'we needs must hear anon
Of him, and of that other.' 'Ay,' she said,
'And of that other, for I needs must hence
And find that other, wheresoe'er he be,
And with mine own hand give his diamond to him,   755
Lest I be found as faithless in the quest
As yon proud Prince who left the quest to me.
Sweet father, I behold him in my dreams
Gaunt as it were the skeleton of himself,
Death-pale, for lack of gentle maiden's aid.   760
The gentler-born the maiden, the more bound,
My father, to be sweet and serviceable
To noble knights in sickness, as ye know

84 Hence bitter as wormwood to the taste.

When these have worn their tokens:[85] let me hence
765 I pray you.' Then her father nodding said,
'Ay, ay, the diamond: wit[86] ye well, my child,
Right fain[87] were I to learn this knight were whole,[88]
Being our greatest: yea, and you must give it —
And sure I think this fruit is hung too high
770 For any mouth to gape for save a queen's —
Nay, I mean nothing: so then, get you gone,
Being so very wilful you must go.'

Lightly, her suit allow'd,[89] she slipt away,
And while she made her ready for her ride,
775 Her father's latest word humm'd in her ear,
'Being so very wilful you must go,'
And changed itself and echo'd in her heart,
'Being so very wilful you must die.'
But she was happy enough and shook it off,
780 As we shake off the bee that buzzes at us;
And in her heart she answer'd it and said,
'What matter, so I help him back to life?'
Then far away with good Sir Torre for guide
Rode o'er the long backs of the bushless downs
785 To Camelot, and before the city-gates
Came on her brother with a happy face
Making a roan horse caper and curvet[90]

[85] By wearing her token, he had fought for her. She must not
help him in distress.
[86] Know.
[87] Happy, glad.
[88] Well and sound.
[89] Request granted.
[90] Leap.

'or pleasure all about a field of flowers:
Whom when she saw, 'Lavaine,' she cried, 'Lavaine,
Iow fares my lord Sir Lancelot?' He amazed,   790
Torre and Elaine! why here? Sir Lancelot!
Iow know ye my lord's name is Lancelot?'
But when the maid had told him all her tale,
Then turn'd Sir Torre, and being in his moods
Left them, and under the strange-statued gate,   795
Where Arthur's wars were render'd mystically,
Past up the still rich city to his kin,
Iis own far blood, which dwelt at Camelot;
And her, Lavaine across the poplar grove
Led to the caves: there first she saw the casque[91]   800
Of Lancelot on the wall: her scarlet sleeve,
Tho' carved and cut, and half the pearls away,
Stream'd from it still; and in her heart she laugh'd,
Because he had not loosed it from his helm,
But meant once more perchance to tourney in it.   805
And when they gain'd the cell wherein he slept,
Iis battle-writhen[92] arms and mighty hands
Lay naked on the wolfskin, and a dream
Of dragging down his enemy made them move.
Then she that saw him lying unsleek, unshorn,   810
Gaunt as it were the skeleton of himself,
Utter'd a little tender dolorous cry.[93]
The sound not wonted in a place so still
Woke the sick knight, and while he roll'd his eyes
Yet blank from sleep, she started to him, saying,   815

[91] Helmet, armor head-piece.
[92] Distorted by the pain of battle.
[93] Cry of grief.

'Your prize the diamond sent you by the King:'
His eyes glisten'd: she fancied 'Is it for me?'
And when the maid had told him all the tale
Of King and Prince, the diamond sent, the quest
820 Assign'd to her not worthy of it, she knelt
Full lowly by the corners of his bed,
And laid the diamond in his open hand.
Her face was near, and as we kiss the child
That does the task assign'd, he kiss'd her face.
825 At once she slipt like water to the floor.
'Alas,' he said, 'your ride hath wearied you.
Rest must you have.' 'No rest for me,' she said;
'Nay, for near you, fair lord, I am at rest.'
What might she mean by that? his large black eyes,
830 Yet larger thro' his leanness, dwelt upon her,
Till all her heart's sad secret blazed itself
In the heart's colours on her simple face;
And Lancelot look'd and was perplext in mind,
And being weak in body said no more;
835 But did not love the colour; woman's love,
Save one, he not regarded, and so turn'd
Sighing, and feign'd[94] a sleep until he slept.

Then rose Elaine and glided thro' the fields,
And past beneath the weirdly-sculptured gates
840 Far up the dim rich city to her kin;
There bode the night: but woke with dawn, and
        past
Down thro' the dim rich city to the fields,
Thence to the cave: so day by day she past

[94] Pretended.

n either twilight ghost-like to and fro
Gliding, and every day she tended him.   845
And likewise many a night: and Lancelot
Would, tho' he call'd his wound a little hurt
Whereof he should be quickly whole, at times
Brain-feverous in his heat and agony, seem
Uncourteous, even he: but the meek maid   850
Sweetly forebore[95] him ever, being to him
Meeker than any child to a rough nurse,
Milder than any mother to a sick child,
And never woman yet, since man's first fall,
Did kindlier unto man, but her deep love   855
Upbore her; till the hermit, skill'd in all
The simples[96] and the science of that time,
Told him that her fine care had saved his life.
And the sick man forgot her simple blush,
Would call her friend and sister, sweet Elaine,   860
Would listen for her coming and regret
Her parting step, and held her tenderly,
And loved her with all love except the love
Of man and woman when they love their best,
Closest and sweetest, and had died the death   865
In any knightly fashion for her sake.
And peradventure had he seen her first
She might have made this and that other world[97]
Another world for the sick man; but now
The shackles of an old love straiten'd[98] him,   870

[95] Bore with him.
[96] Medicinal herbs and plants.
[97] Earth and heaven.
[98] Bound him.

His honour rooted in dishonour stood,
And faith unfaithful kept him falsely true.

 Yet the great knight in his mid-sickness[99] made
Full many a holy vow and pure resolve.
875 These, as but born of sickness, could not live:
For when the blood ran lustier in him again,
Full often the bright image of one face,[100]
Making a treacherous quiet in his heart,
Dispersed his resolution like a cloud.
880 Then if the maiden, while that ghostly grace[101]
Beam'd on his fancy, spoke, he answer'd not,
Or short and coldly, and she knew right well
What the rough sickness meant, but what this meant
She knew not, and the sorrow dimm'd her sight,
885 And drave her ere her time across the fields
Far into the rich city, where alone
She murmur'd, 'Vain, in vain: it cannot be.
He will not love me: how then? must I die?'
Then as a little helpless innocent bird,
890 That has but one plain passage of few notes,
Will sing the simple passage o'er and o'er
For all an April morning, till the ear
Wearies to hear it, so the simple maid
Went half the night repeating, 'Must I die?'
895 And now to right she turn'd, and now to left,
And found no ease in turning or in rest;
And 'Him or death,' she mutter'd, 'death or him,'

99 In the midst of his sickness.
100 Guinevere.
101 While the heavy mood was upon him.

Again and like a burthen, 'Him or death.'

But when Sir Lancelot's deadly hurt was whole,
To Astolat returning rode the three.   900
There morn by morn, arraying her sweet self
In that wherein she deem'd she look'd her best,
She came before Sir Lancelot, for she thought
'If I be loved, these are my festal robes,
If not, the victim's flowers before he fall.'   905
And Lancelot ever prest upon the maid
That she should ask some goodly gift of him
For her own self or hers; 'and do not shun
To speak the wish most near to your true heart;
Such service have ye done me, that I make   910
My will of yours, and Prince and Lord am I
In mine own land, and while I will I can.'
Then like a ghost she lifted up her face,
But like a ghost without the power to speak.
And Lancelot saw that she withheld her wish,   915
And bode among them yet a little space
Till he should learn it; and one morn it chanced
He found her in among the garden yews,
And said, 'Delay no longer, speak your wish,
Seeing I go to-day:' then out she brake: 920
'Going? and we shall never see you more.
And I must die for want of one bold word.'
'Speak: that I live to hear,' he said, 'is yours.'[102]
Then suddenly and passionately she spoke:
'I have gone mad. I love you: let me die.'   925
'Ah, sister,' answer'd Lancelot, 'what is this?'

[102] That I am alive to hear is due to your care.

And innocently extending her white arms,
'Your love,' she said, 'your love — to be your wife.'
And Lancelot answer'd, 'Had I chosen to wed,
930 I had been wedded earlier, sweet Elaine:
But now there never will be wife of mine.'
'No, no,' she cried, 'I care not to be wife,
But to be with you still, to see your face,
To serve you, and to follow you thro' the world.'
935 And Lancelot answer'd, 'Nay, the world, the world,
All ear and eye, with such a stupid heart
To interpret ear and eye, and such a tongue
To blare its own interpretation — nay,
Full ill then should I quit[103] your brother's love,
940 And your father's kindness.' And she said,
'Not to be with you, not to see your face —
Alas for me then, my good days are done.'
'Nay, noble maid,' he answer'd, 'ten times nay!
This is not love: but love's first flash in youth,
945 Most common: yea, I know it of mine own self:
And you yourself will smile at your own self
Hereafter, when you yield your flower of life
To one more fitly yours, not thrice your age:
And then will I, for true you are and sweet
950 Beyond mine old belief in womanhood,
More specially should your good knight be poor,
Endow you with broad land and territory
Even to the half my realm beyond the seas,
So that would make you happy: furthermore,
955 Ev'n to the death, as tho' ye were my blood,[104]

[103] Very badly should I reward your brother's love.
[104] One of my family.

a all your quarrels will I be your knight.
'his will I do, dear damsel, for your sake,
nd more than this I cannot.'

           While he spoke
he neither blush'd nor shook, but deathly-pale
tood grasping what was nearest, then replied: 960
Of all this will I nothing;' and so fell,
nd thus they bore her swooning to her **tower.**

  Then spake, to whom thro' those black walls of yew
'heir talk had pierced, her father: 'Ay, a flash,
fear me, that will strike my blossom dead.   965
'oo courteous are ye, fair Lord Lancelot.
pray you, use some rough discourtesy
'o blunt or break her passion.'

           Lancelot said,
That were against me: what I can I will;'
nd there that day remain'd, and toward even   970
ent for his shield: full meekly rose the maid,
tript off the case, and gave the naked shield;
'hen, when she heard his horse upon the stones,
Unclasping flung the casement back, and look'd
Down on his helm, from which her sleeve had gone.   975
nd Lancelot knew the little clinking sound;
nd she by tact of love[105] was well aware
'hat Lancelot knew that she was looking at him.
nd yet he glanced not up, nor waved his hand,
'or bade farewell, but sadly rode away.   980
'his was the one discourtesy that he used.

[105] Feeling or insight.

So in her tower alone the maiden sat:
His very shield was gone; only the case,
Her own poor work, her empty labour, left.
985 But still she heard him, still his picture form'd
And grew between her and the pictured wall.
Then came her father, saying in low tones,
'Have comfort,' whom she greeted quietly.
Then came her brethren saying, 'Peace to thee,
990 Sweet sister,' whom she answer'd with all calm.
But when they left her to herself again,
Death, like a friend's voice from a distant field
Approaching thro' the darkness, call'd; the owls
Wailing had power upon her, and she mixt
995 Her fancies with the sallow-rifted glooms[106]
Of evening, and the moanings of the wind.

And in those days she made a little song,
And call'd her song 'The Song of Love and Death,'
And sang it: sweetly could she make and sing.

1000   'Sweet is true love tho' given in vain, in vain;
And sweet is death who puts an end to pain:
I know not which is sweeter, no, not I.

'Love, art thou sweet? then bitter death must be:
Love, thou art bitter; sweet is death to me.
1005 O Love, if death be sweeter, let me die.

'Sweet love, that seems not made to fade away,
Sweet death, that seems to make us loveless clay,
I know not which is sweeter, no, not I.

106 Heavy clouds with rifts of light.

'I fain would follow love, if that could be;
I needs must follow death, who calls for me;   1011
Call and I follow, I follow! let me die.'

High with the last line scaled her voice, and this,
All in a fiery dawning wild with wind
That shook her tower, the brothers heard, and thought
With shuddering, 'Hark the Phantom of the house[107] 1015
That ever shrieks before a death,' and call'd
The father, and all three in hurry and fear
Ran to her, and lo! the blood-red light of dawn
Flared on her face, she shrilling, 'Let me die!'

As when we dwell upon a word we know,   1020
Repeating, till the word we know so well
Becomes a wonder, and we know not why,
So dwelt the father on her face, and thought
'Is this Elaine?' till back the maiden fell,
Then gave a languid hand to each, and lay,   1025
Speaking a still good-morrow with her eyes.
At last she said, 'Sweet brothers, yesternight
I seem'd a curious[108] little maid again,
As happy as when we dwelt among the woods,
And when ye used to take me with the flood   1030
Up the great river in the boatman's boat.
Only ye would not pass beyond the cape
That has the poplar on it: there ye fixt

[107] An allusion to the Banshee, a female spectre, who, according to
Celtic tradition, always appeared and lamented when a member of
the household was about to die.
[108] Simple inquisitive maiden.

Your limit, oft returning with the tide.
1035 And yet I cried because ye would not pass
Beyond it, and far up the shining flood
Until we found the palace of the King.
And yet ye would not; but this night I dream'd
That I was all alone upon the flood,
1040 And then I said, "Now shall I have my will:"
And there I woke, but still the wish remain'd.
So let me hence that I may pass at last
Beyond the poplar and far up the flood,
Until I find the palace of the King.
1045 There will I enter in among them all,
And no man there will dare to mock at me;
But there the fine Gawain will wonder at me,
And there the great Sir Lancelot muse[109] at me;
Gawain, who bade a thousand farewells to me,
1050 Lancelot, who coldly went, nor bade me one:
And there the King will know me and my love,
And there the Queen herself will pity me,
And all the gentle court will welcome me,
And after my long voyage I shall rest!'

1055   'Peace,' said her father, 'O my child, ye seem
Light-headed, for what force[110] is yours to go
So far, being sick? and wherefore would ye look
On this proud fellow again, who scorns us all?'

    Then the rough Torre began to heave and move,
1060 And bluster into stormy sobs and say,

[109] Wonder.
,   [110] What strength have you.

'I never loved him: an I meet with him,
I care not howsoever great he be,
Then will I strike at him and strike him down,
Give me good fortune, I will strike him dead,
For this discomfort he hath done the house.'   1065

To whom the gentle sister made reply,
'Fret not yourself, dear brother, nor be wroth,[111]
Seeing it is no more Sir Lancelot's fault
Not to love me, than it is mine to love
Him of all men who seems to me the highest.'   1070

'Highest?' the father answer'd, echoing 'highest?'
(He meant to break the passion in her) 'nay,
Daughter, I know not what you call the highest;
But this I know, for all the people know it,
He loves the Queen, and in an open shame: 1075
And she returns his love in open shame;
If this be high, what is it to be low?'

Then spake the lily maid of Astolat:
'Sweet father, all too faint and sick am I
For anger: these are slanders: never yet   1080
Was noble man but made ignoble talk.
He makes no friend who never made a foe.
But now it is my glory to have loved
One peerless,[112] without stain: so let me pass,
My father, howsoe'er I seem to you,   1085
Not all unhappy, having loved God's best

[111] Angry.
[112] Without a peer, unequaled.

And greatest, tho' my love had no return:
Yet, seeing you desire your child to live,
Thanks, but you work against your own desire;
1090 For if I could believe the things you say
I should but die the sooner; wherefore cease,
Sweet father, and bid call the ghostly man[113]
Hither, and let me shrive[114] me clean, and die.'

So when the ghostly man had come and gone,
1095 She with a face, bright as for sin forgiven,
Besought Lavaine to write as she devised
A letter, word for word; and when he ask'd
'Is it for Lancelot, is it for my dear lord?'
Then will I bear it gladly;' she replied,
1100 'For Lancelot and the Queen and all the world,
But I myself must bear it.' Then he wrote
The letter she devised; which being writ
And folded, 'O sweet father, tender and true,
Deny me not,' she said — 'ye never yet
1105 Denied my fancies — this, however strange,
My latest: lay the letter in my hand
A little ere I die, and close the hand
Upon it; I shall guard it even in death.
And when the heat is gone from out my heart
1110 Then take the little bed on which I died
For Lancelot's love, and deck[115] it like the Queen's
For richness, and me also like the Queen
In all I have of rich, and lay me on it.

[113] The priest.
[114] Make confession and receive absolution preparatory to death.
[115] Decorate it.

And let there be prepared a chariot-bier[116]
To take me to the river, and a barge   1115
Be ready on the river, clothed in black.
I go in state to court, to meet the Queen.
There surely I shall speak for mine own self,
And none of you can speak for me so well.
And therefore let our dumb old man alone   1120
Go with me, he can steer and row, and he
Will guide me to that palace, to the doors.'

She ceased: her father promised; whereupon
She grew so cheerful that they deem'd her death
Was rather in the fantasy than the blood.   1125
But ten slow mornings past, and on the eleventh
Her father laid the letter in her hand,
And closed the hand upon it, and she died.
So that day there was dole[117] in Astolat.

But when the next sun brake from underground,   1130
Then, those two brethren slowly with bent brows,
Accompanying, the sad chariot-bier
Past like a shadow thro' the field, that shone
Full-summer, to that stream whereon the barge,
Pall'd[118] all its length in blackest samite, lay.   1135
There sat the lifelong creature of the house,
Loyal, the dumb old servitor,[119] on deck,
Winking his eyes, and twisted all his face,

[116] Funeral-wagon, forerunner of the hearse.
[117] Heavy grief.
[118] Covered by a pall of heavy black silk.
[119] Servant.

So those two brethren from the chariot took
1140 And on the black decks laid her in her bed,
Set in her hand a lily, o'er her hung
The silken case with braided blazonings,
And kiss'd her quiet brows, and saying to her,
'Sister, farewell for ever,' and again
1145 'Farewell, sweet sister,' parted all in tears.
Then rose the dumb old servitor, and the dead,
Oar'd by the dumb, went upward with the flood —
In her right hand the lily, in her left
The letter — all her bright hair streaming down —
1150 And all the coverlid was cloth of gold
Drawn to her waist, and she herself in white
All but her face, and that clear-featured face
Was lovely, for she did not seem as dead,
But fast asleep, and lay as tho' she smiled.

1155   That day Sir Lancelot at the palace craved
Audience of Guinevere, to give at last
The price of half a realm, his costly gift,
Hard-won and hardly won with bruise and blow,
With deaths of others, and almost his own,
1160 The nine-years-fought-for diamonds: for he saw
One of her house, and sent him to the Queen
Bearing his wish, whereto the Queen agreed
With such and so unmoved a majesty
She might have seem'd her statue, but that he,
1165 Low-drooping[120] till he wellnigh kiss'd her feet
For loyal awe, saw with a sidelong eye
The shadow of some piece of pointed lace,

[120] Bowing low.

In the Queen's shadow, vibrate on the walls,
And parted, laughing in his courtly heart.

All in an oriel[121] on the summer side,[122]   1170
Vine-clad, of Arthur's palace toward the stream,
They met, and Lancelot kneeling utter'd, 'Queen,
Lady, my liege,[123] in whom I have my joy,
Take, what I had not won except for you,
These jewels, and make me happy, making them   1175
An armlet for the roundest arm on earth,
Or necklace for a neck to which the swan's
Is tawnier than her cygnet's:[124] these are words:
Your beauty is your beauty, and I sin
In speaking, yet O grant my worship of it   1180
Words, as we grant grief tears. Such sin in words
Perchance, we both can pardon: but, my Queen,
I hear of rumours flying thro' your court.
Our bond, as not the bond of man and wife,
Should have in it an absoluter trust   1185
To make up that defect: let rumours be:
When did not rumours fly? these, as I trust
That you trust me in your own nobleness,
I may not well believe that you believe.'

While thus he spoke, half-turn'd away, the Queen   1190
Brake from the vast oriel-embowering vine
Leaf after leaf, and tore, and cast them off,

[121] A window built out from the wall.
[122] South.
[123] My Sovereign.
[124] The young swan.

Till all the place whereon she stood was green;
Then, when he ceased, in one cold passive hand
1195 Received at once and laid aside the gems
There on a table near her, and replied:

'It may be, I am quicker of belief
Than you believe me,[125] Lancelot of the Lake.
Our bond is not the bond of man and wife.
1200 This good is in it, whatsoe'er of ill,
It can be broken easier. I for you
This many a year have done despite and wrong
To one whom ever in my heart of hearts
I did acknowledge nobler. What are these?
1205 Diamonds for me! they had been thrice their worth
Being your gift, had you not lost your own.[126]
To loyal hearts the value of all gifts
Must vary as the giver's. Not for me!
For her! for your new fancy.[127] Only this
1210 Grant me, I pray you: have your joys apart.[128]
I doubt not that however changed, you keep
So much of what is graceful: and myself
Would shun to break those bounds of courtesy
In which as Arthur's Queen I move and rule:
1215 So cannot speak my mind. An end to this!
A strange one! yet I take it with Amen.[129]
So pray you, add my diamonds to her pearls;

[125] It may be that I believe rumors quicker than you think.
[126] Your own worth to me.
[127] Your new love.
[128] Apart from me.
[129] With resignation.

Deck her with these; tell her she shines me down.[130]
An armlet for an arm to which the Queen's
Is haggard, or a necklace for a neck   1220
O as much fairer — as a faith once fair
Was richer than these diamonds — hers not mine —
Nay, by the mother of our Lord himself,[131]
Or hers or mine, mine now to work my will —
She shall not have them.'

                Saying which she seized,   1225
And, thro' the casement,[132] standing wide for heat,
Flung them, and down they flash'd, and smote the
      stream.
Then from the smitten surface flash'd, as it were,
Diamonds to meet them, and they past away.
Then while Sir Lancelot leant, in half disdain   1230
At love, life, all things, on the window ledge,
Close underneath his eyes, and right across
Where these had fallen, slowly past the barge
Whereon the lily maid of Astolat
Lay smiling, like a star in blackest night.   1235

    But the wild Queen, who saw not, burst away
To weep and wail in secret; and the barge,
On to the palace-doorway sliding, paused.
There two stood arm'd, and kept the door; to whom,
All up the marble stair, tier over tier,   1240
Were added mouths that gaped, and eyes that ask'd

[130] She has won preferment over me.
[131] A common form of oath, by the Virgin Mary.
[132] The open window.

'What is it?' but that oarsman's haggard face,
As hard and still as is the face that men
Shape to their fancy's eye from broken rocks
1245 On some cliff-side, appall'd them, and they said,
'He is enchanted, cannot speak — and she,
Look how she sleeps — the Fairy Queen, so fair!
Yea, but how pale! what[133] are they? flesh and blood?
Or come to take the King to Fairyland?
1250 For some do hold our Arthur cannot die,
But that he passes into Fairyland.'

While thus they babbled of the King, the King
Came girt[134] with knights: then turn'd the tongueless
       man
From the half-face to the full eye,[135] and rose
1255 And pointed to the damsel, and the doors.
So Arthur bade the meek Sir Percivale
And pure Sir Galahad[136] to uplift the maid;
And reverently they bore her into hall.
Then came the fine Gawain and wonder'd at her,
1260 And Lancelot later came and mused at her,
And last the Queen herself, and pitied her:
But Arthur spied the letter in her hand,
Stoopt, took, brake seal, and read it; this was all:

'Most noble lord, Sir Lancelot of the Lake,
1265 I, sometime call'd the maid of Astolat,

[133] Who.
[134] Surrounded.
[135] From profile to full face.
[136] Sir Percivale and Sir Galahad were the most pure and holy of
King Arthur's knights.

Come, for you left me taking no farewell,
Hither, to take my last farewell of you.
I loved you, and my love had no return,
And therefore my true love has been my death.
And therefore to our Lady Guinevere, 1270
And to all other ladies, I make moan:
Pray for my soul, and yield me burial.
Pray for my soul thou too, Sir Lancelot,
As thou art a knight peerless.'

Thus he read;
And ever in the reading, lords and dames 1275
Wept, looking often from his face who read
To hers which lay so silent, and at times,
So touch'd were they, half-thinking that her lips,
Who had devised the letter,[137] moved again.
Then freely spoke Sir Lancelot to them all: 1280
'My lord liege Arthur, and all ye that hear,
Know that for this most gentle maiden's death
Right heavy[138] am I; for good she was and true,
But loved me with a love beyond all love
In women, whomsoever I have known. 1285
Yet to be loved makes not to love again;
Not at my years, however it hold in youth.
I swear by truth and knighthood that I gave
No cause, not willingly, for such a love:
To this I call my friends in testimony, 1290
Her brethren, and her father, who himself

[137] The lips of her who had devised the letter.
[138] Right sorrowful.

Besought me to be plain and blunt, and use,
To break her passion, some discourtesy
Against my nature: what I could, I did.
295 I left her and I bade her no farewell;
Tho', had I dreamt the damsel would have died,
I might have put my wits to some rough use[139]
And help'd her from herself.'

                              Then said the Queen
(Sea was her wrath, yet working after storm),
1300 'Ye might at least have done her so much grace,
Fair lord, as would have help'd[140] her from her death.'
He raised his head, their eyes met and hers fell,
He adding,

                    'Queen, she would not be content
Save that I wedded her, which could not be.
1305 Then might she follow me thro' the world, she ask'd;
It could not be. I told her that her love
Was but the flash of youth, would darken down
To rise hereafter in a stiller flame
Toward one more worthy of her — then would I,
1310 More specially were he, she wedded, poor,
Estate[141] them with large land and territory
In mine own realm beyond the narrow seas,[142]
To keep them in all joyance: more than this
I could not; this she would not, and she died.'

[139] More active use.
[140] Kept her from her death.
[141] Endow.
[142] English Channel.

He pausing, Arthur answer'd, 'O my knight,   1315
It will be to thy worship,[143] as my knight,
And mine, as head of all our Table Round,
To see that she be buried worshipfully.'[144]

So toward that shrine[145] which then in all the realm
Was richest, Arthur leading, slowly went   1320
The marshall'd Order of their Table Round,
And Lancelot sad beyond his wont, to see
The maiden buried, not as one unknown,
Not meanly, but with gorgeous obsequies,
And mass, and rolling music, like a queen.   1325
And when the knights had laid her comely head
Low in the dust of half-forgotten kings,[146]
Then Arthur spake among them, 'Let her tomb
Be costly, and her image thereupon,
And let the shield of Lancelot at her feet   1330
Be carven, and her lily in her hand.
And let the story of her dolorous voyage
For all true hearts be blazon'd on her tomb
In letters gold and azure!' which was wrought
Thereafter; but when now the lords and dames   1335
And people, from the high door streaming, brake
Disorderly, as homeward each, the Queen,
Who mark'd Sir Lancelot where he moved apart,
Drew near, and sigh'd in passing, 'Lancelot,
Forgive me; mine was jealousy in love.'   1340

[143] Credit and honor.
[144] In a manner worthy of her rank.
[145] Westminster, where only the most honored ones were buried.
[146] Westminster Abbey was the burial place of the Kings.

He answer'd with his eyes upon the ground,
'That is love's curse; pass on, my Queen, forgiven.'
But Arthur, who beheld his cloudy brows,
Approach'd him, and with full affection said,

1345   'Lancelot, my Lancelot, thou in whom I have
Most joy and most affiance,[147] for I know
What thou hast been in battle by my side,
And many a time have watch'd thee at the tilt
Strike down the lusty and long-practised knight,
1350 And let the younger and unskill'd go by
To win his honour and to make his name,
And loved thy courtesies and thee, a man
Made to be loved; but now I would to God,
Seeing the homeless trouble in thine eyes,
1355 Thou couldst have loved this maiden, shaped, it seems,
By God for thee alone, and from her face,
If one may judge the living by the dead,
Delicately pure and marvellously fair,
Who might have brought thee, now a lonely man
1360 Wifeless and heirless, noble issue, sons
Born to the glory of thy name and fame,
My knight, the great Sir Lancelot of the Lake.'

Then answer'd Lancelot, 'Fair she was, my King,
Pure, as you ever wish your knights to be.
1365 To doubt her fairness were to want an eye,
To doubt her pureness were to want a heart —
Yea, to be loved, if what is worthy love
Could bind him, but free love will not be bound.'

   [147] Confidence, trust.

'Free love, so bound, were freëst,' said the King.
Let love be free; free love is for the best: 1370
And, after heaven, on our dull side of death,
What should be best, if not so pure a love
Clothed in so pure a loveliness? yet thee
She fail'd to bind, tho' being, as I think,
Unbound as yet, and gentle, as I know.'   1375

     And Lancelot answer'd nothing, but he went,
And at the inrunning of a little brook
Sat by the river in a cove, and watch'd
The high reed wave, and lifted up his eyes
And saw the barge that brought her moving down,   1380
Far-off, a blot upon the stream, and said
Low in himself, 'Ah, simple heart and sweet,
Ye loved me, damsel, surely with a love
Far tenderer than my Queen's. Pray for thy soul?
Ay, that will I. Farewell too — now at last —   1385
Farewell, fair lily. "Jealousy in love?"
Not rather dead love's harsh heir, jealous pride?
Queen, if I grant the jealousy as of love,
May not your crescent[148] fear for name and fame
Speak, as it waxes,[149] of a love that wanes?   1390
Why did the King dwell on my name to me?
Mine own name shames me, seeming a reproach,
Lancelot, whom the Lady of the Lake
Caught from his mother's arms — the wondrous one
Who passes thro' the vision of the night —   1395
She chanted snatches of mysterious hymns

[148] Growing.
[149] Grows or increases.

Heard on the winding waters, eve and morn
She kiss'd me saying, "Thou art fair, my child,
As a king's son," and often in her arms
1400 She bare me, pacing on the dusky mere.
Would she had drown'd me in it, where'er it be!
For what am I? what profits me my name
Of greatest knight? I fought for it, and have it:
Pleasure to have it, none; to lose it, pain;
1405 Now grown a part of me: but what use in it?
To make men worse by making my sin known?
Or sin seem less, the sinner seeming great?
Alas for Arthur's greatest knight, a man
Not after Arthur's heart! I needs must break
1410 These bonds that so defame me: not without
She[150] wills it: would I, if she will'd it? nay,
Who knows? but if I would not, then may God,
I pray him, send a sudden Angel down
To seize me by the hair and bear me far,
1415 And fling me deep in that forgotten mere,[151]
Among the tumbled fragments of the hills.'

So groan'd Sir Lancelot in remorseful pain,
Not knowing he should die a holy man.[152]

[150] Guinevere (gwĭn'ê-vēr).
[151] The lake where dwelt the Lady of the Lake.
[152] Malory tells how Lancelot later served God in a monastery doing penance six years before his death.

THE HOLY GRAIL[1]

From noiseful arms, and acts of prowess done
In tournament or tilt, Sir Percivale,[2]
Whom Arthur and his knighthood call'd The Pure,
Had pass'd into the silent life of prayer,[3]
Praise, fast, and alms; and leaving for the cowl[4]   5
The helmet in an abbey[5] far away
From Camelot, there, and not long after, died.

And one, a fellow-monk among the rest,
Ambrosius,[6] loved him much beyond the rest,
And honor'd him, and wrought into his heart   10
A way by love that waken'd love within,
To answer that which came: and as they sat
Beneath a world-old yew-tree, darkening half

[1] The cup from which Jesus and the disciples drank at the Last Supper. Legend has it that the Holy Grail was carried by Joseph of Arimathea to Glastonbury whence it disappeared never again to be seen save by those who were pure in heart.

[2] Percivale is the central figure in the best known versions of the Holy Grail and in Wagner's opera, *Parsifal*.

[3] After his career as a knight, he retired to a monastery for prayer and meditation, as was the custom in days of knighthood.

[4] The hood of a monk as contrasted with *helmet*, the head-gear of the knight.

[5] Monastery in which the monks are governed by an abbot.

[6] Ambrosius was an uneducated, simple-minded monk who had known only the life of the monastery. He is contrasted to Sir Percivale, the knight of heroic adventures, acquainted with courts and kings.

The cloisters,[7] on a gustful April morn
15 That puff'd the swaying branches into smoke
Above them, ere the summer when he died,
The monk Ambrosius question'd Percivale:

'O brother, I have seen this yew-tree smoke,[8]
Spring after spring, for half a hundred years:
20 For never have I known the world without,
Nor ever stray'd beyond the pale:[9] but thee,
When first thou camest—such a courtesy
Spake thro' the limbs and in the voice[10]—I knew
For one of those who eat in Arthur's hall;
25 For good ye are and bad, and like to coins,
Some true, some light, but every one of you
Stamp'd with the image of the King; and now
Tell me, what drove thee from the Table Round,
My brother? was it earthly passion crost?'[11]

30   'Nay,' said the knight;[12] 'for no such passion mine.
But the sweet vision of the Holy Grail
Drove me from all vainglories, rivalries,
And earthly heats that spring and sparkle out
Among us in the jousts, while women watch

[7] The closed court within the monastery, usually with a garden surrounded by an arch-covered walk or work spaces.

[8] The pollen dust of the yew-tree scattered by the wind.

[9] The walls, or boundaries, of the monastery.

[10] Sir Percivale's bearing showed that he was a superior knight.

[11] Was it thwarted earthly ambition?

[12] The remainder of *The Holy Grail* takes the form of a dialogue between the monk Ambrosius as questioner and Sir Percivale as narrator of the story.

Who wins, who falls; and waste the spiritual strength   35
Within us, better offer'd up to Heaven.'

  To whom the monk: 'The Holy Grail!—I trust
We are green[13] in Heaven's eyes; but here too much
We molder—as to things without I mean—
Yet one of your own knights, a guest of ours,   40
Told us of this in our refectory,[14]
But spake with such a sadness and so low
We heard not half of what he said. What is it?
The phantom of a cup that comes and goes?'

  'Nay, monk! what phantom?' answer'd Percivale.   45
The cup, the cup itself, from which our Lord
Drank at the last sad supper with his own.
This, from the blessed land of Aromat[15]—
After the day of darkness, when the dead
Went wandering o'er Moriah[16]—the good saint   50
Arimathæan Joseph, journeying brought
To Glastonbury, where the winter thorn
Blossoms at Christmas, mindful of our Lord.
And there awhile it bode;[17] and if a man
Could touch or see, he was heal'd at once,   55
By faith, of all his ills. But then the times

[13] Gifted with life, though seeming dead from an earthly stand-point.
[14] The dining room of a monastery.
[15] Arimathea, a village in Judea.
[16] See Matt. XXVII, 52-3. Moriah was the mountain in Jerusalem upon which the Temple was built.
[17] Remained.

Grew to such evil that the holy cup
Was caught away to Heaven, and disappear'd.'

    To whom the monk: 'From our old books I know
60 That Joseph came of old to Glastonbury,
And there the heathen Prince, Arviragus,[18]
Gave him an isle of marsh whereon to build;
And there he built with wattles[19] from the marsh
A little lonely church in days of yore,
65 For so they say, these books of ours, but seem
Mute of this miracle,[20] far as I have read.
But who first saw the holy thing to-day?'[21]

    'A woman,' answer'd Percivale, 'a nun,
And one no further off in blood from me
70 Than sister; and if ever holy maid
With knees of adoration wore the stone,[22]
A holy maid; tho' never maiden glow'd,
But that was in her earlier maidenhood,
With such a fervent flame of human love,
75 Which being rudely blunted, glanced and shot
Only to holy things; to prayer and praise
She gave herself, to fast and alms. And yet,
Nun as she was, the scandal of the Court,
Sin against Arthur and the Table Round,
80 And the strange sound of an adulterous race,

[18] One of the sons of Cymbeline, immortalized by Shakespear
and an ancient King of Britain from 44 to 72 A.D.

[19] Plaited or woven reeds or twigs.

[20] Silent about the Holy Grail.

[21] In the present age.

[22] Wore the stone before the altar by kneeling in prayer.

Across the iron grating of her cell
Beat, and she pray'd and fasted all the more.

'And he[23] to whom she told her sins, or what
Her all but utter whiteness held for sin,
A man wellnigh a hundred winters old,   85
Spake often with her of the Holy Grail,
A legend handed down thro' five or six,
And each of these a hundred winters old,
From our Lord's time. And when King Arthur made
His Table Round, and all men's hearts became   90
Clean for a season, surely he had thought
That now the Holy Grail would come again;
But sin broke out. Ah, Christ, that it would come,
And heal the world of all their wickedness!
'O Father!" ask'd the maiden, "might it come   95
To me by prayer and fasting?" "Nay," said he,
'I know not, for thy heart is pure as snow."
And so she pray'd and fasted, till the sun
Shone, and the wind blew, thro' her,[24] and I thought
She might have risen and floated when I saw her.   100

'For on a day she sent to speak with me.
And when she came to speak, behold her eyes
Beyond my knowing of them, beautiful,
Beyond all knowing of them, wonderful,
Beautiful in the light of holiness.   105
And "O my brother Percivale," she said,
'Sweet brother, I have seen the Holy Grail:

[23] A priest, her father confessor.
[24] Because of her faith and prayers.

For, waked at dead of night, I heard a sound
As of a silver horn from o'er the hills
110 Blown, and I thought, 'It is not Arthur's use[25]
To hunt by moonlight'; and the slender sound
As from a distance beyond distance grew
Coming upon me—O never harp nor horn,
Nor aught we blow with breath, or touch with hand,
115 Was like that music as it came; and then
Stream'd thro' my cell a cold and silver beam,
And down the long beam stole the Holy Grail,
Rose-red with beatings[26] in it, as if alive,
Till all the white walls of my cell were dyed
120 With rosy colors leaping[27] on the wall;
And then the music faded, and the Grail
Past, and the beam decay'd, and from the walls
The rosy quiverings died into the night.
So now the Holy Thing is here again
125 Among us, brother, fast thou too and pray,
And tell thy brother knights to fast and pray,
That so perchance the vision may be seen
By thee and those, and all the world be heal'd."

'Then leaving the pale nun, I spake of this
130 To all men; and myself fasted and pray'd
Always, and many among us many a week
Fasted and pray'd even to the uttermost,

[25] Custom.

[26] See also lines 473–6. According to the ancient legend, Joseph of Arimathea collected the blood of Jesus in the Holy Grail, hence *rose-red* and *blood-red*.

[27] Quivering, as if reflected from the surface of a slightly-moving liquid.

xpectant of the wonder that would be.

'And one there was among us, ever moved
mong us in white armor, Galahad.[28]   135
God make thee good as thou art beautiful,"
aid Arthur, when he dubb'd him knight;[29] and none
a so young youth,[30] was ever made a knight
ill Galahad; and this Galahad, when he heard
Ty sister's vision, fill'd me with amaze;   140
is eyes became so like her own, they seem'd
ers, and himself her brother more than I.

'Sister or brother none had he; but some
all'd him a son of Lancelot, and some said
egotten by enchantment—chatterers they,   145
ike birds of passage piping up and down
hat gape for flies—we know not whence they come;
or when was Lancelot wanderingly lewd?

'But she, the wan sweet maiden, shore away
lean from her forehead all that wealth of hair   150
Vhich made a silken mat-work for her feet;
nd out of this she plaited broad and long
strong sword-belt, and wove with silver thread
nd crimson in the belt a strange device,
crimson grail within a silver beam;   155

[28] A knight of youth, beauty, and stainless life.
[29] Dubbing a knight was the act of striking the kneeling warrior
ver the shoulder with the broad side of the sword-blade and saying
I dub thee knight!"
[30] Galahad was dubbed a knight at the age of 15, according to the
gend.

And saw the bright boy-knight, and bound it on him,
Saying, "My knight, my love, my knight of heaven,
O thou, my love, whose love is one with mine,
I, maiden, round thee, maiden,[31] bind my belt.
160 Go forth, for thou shalt see what I have seen,
And break thro' all, till one will crown thee king[32]
Far in the spiritual city": and as she spake
She sent the deathless passion in her eyes
Thro' him, and made him hers, and laid her mind
165 On him, and he believed in her belief.

'Then came a year of miracle: O brother,
In our great hall there stood a vacant chair,
Fashion'd by Merlin ere he past away,
And carven with strange figures; and in and out
170 The figures, like a serpent, ran a scroll[33]
Of letters in a tongue no man could read.
And Merlin call'd it "The Siege perilous,"[34]
Perilous for good and ill; "for there," he said,
"No man could sit but he should lose himself":
175 And once by misadvertence Merlin sat
In his own chair, and so was lost; but he,
Galahad, when he heard of Merlin's doom,
Cried, "If I lose myself, I save myself!"

'Then on a summer night it came to pass,

[31] A maiden knight, or knight setting out on his first great quest.
[32] See line 482.
[33] An ornament in the form of a scroll, or partly unrolled sheet of paper.
[34] The seat perilous. One legend tells us that Merlin by mischance sat in this seat and "past away." Merlin foretold that only one should ever sit in it and live, and that he should see the Holy Grail

While the great banquet lay along the hall,   180
That Galahad would sit down in Merlin's chair.

'And all at once, as there we sat, we heard
A cracking and a riving[35] of the roofs,
And rending, and a blast, and overhead
Thunder, and in the thunder was a cry.   185
And in the blast there smote along the hall
A beam of light seven times[36] more clear than day:
And down the long beam stole the Holy Grail
All over cover'd with a luminous cloud,
And none might see who bare it, and it past.   190
But every knight beheld his fellow's face
As in a glory, and all the knights arose,
And staring each at other like dumb men
Stood, till I found a voice and sware a vow.

'I sware a vow before them all, that I,   195
Because I had not seen the Grail, would ride
A twelvemonth and a day[37] in quest of it,
Until I found and saw it, as the nun
My sister saw it; and Galahad sware the vow,
And good Sir Bors, our Lancelot's cousin,[38] sware,   200
And Lancelot sware, and many among the knights,
And Gawain sware, and louder than the rest.'

Then spake the monk Ambrosius, asking him,
'What said the King? Did Arthur take the vow?'

[35] Splitting.
[36] Seven was regarded as a mystic number.
[37] See *Gareth and Lynette*, line 154.
[38] Kinsman, nephew of Lancelot.

205   'Nay, for my lord,' said Percivale, 'the King,
      Was not in hall: for early that same day
      Scaped thro' a cavern from a bandit hold,[39]
      An outraged maiden sprang into the hall
      Crying on [40] help: for all her shining hair
210 Was smear'd with earth, and either milky arm
      Red-rent with hooks of bramble, and all she wore
      Torn as a sail that leaves the rope is torn
      In tempest: so the King arose and went
      To smoke the scandalous hive of those wild bees
215 That made such honey in his realm. Howbeit
      Some little of this marvel he too saw,
      Returning o'er the plain that then began
      To darken under Camelot;[41] whence the King
      Look'd up, calling aloud, "Lo, there! the roofs
220 Of our great hall are roll'd in thunder-smoke!
      Pray Heaven, they be not smitten by the bolt."
      For dear to Arthur was that hall of ours,
      As having there so oft with all his knights
      Feasted, and as the stateliest under heaven.

225   'O brother, had you known our mighty hall,
      Which Merlin built for Arthur long ago!
      For all the sacred mount of Camelot,
      And all the dim rich city, roof by roof,
      Tower after tower, spire beyond spire,
230 By grove, and garden-lawn, and rushing brook,
      Climbs to the mighty hall that Merlin built.

      [39] Stronghold.
      [40] For.
      [41] Arthur's capital.

And four great zones of sculpture,[42] set betwixt
With many a mystic symbol, gird the hall:
And in the lowest beasts are slaying men,
And in the second men are slaying beasts,   235
And on the third are warriors, perfect men,
And on the fourth are men with growing wings,
And over all one statue in the mold[43]
Of Arthur, made by Merlin, with a crown,
And peak'd wings pointed to the Northern Star.   240
And eastward fronts the statue, and the crown
And both the wings are made of gold, and flame
At sunrise till the people in far fields
Wasted so often by the heathen hordes,
Behold it, crying, "We have still a King."   245

'And, brother, had you known our hall within,
Broader and higher than any in all the lands!
Where twelve great windows blazon Arthur's wars,
And all the light that falls upon the board
Streams thro' the twelve great battles of our King.[44]   250
Nay, one there is, and at the eastern end,
Wealthy with wandering lines of mount and mere,[45]

[42] The outer walls of the great round hall were decorated by four
belts of sculpture representing (1) the savage state of society, (2)
the rising of man above the beast existence, (3) the full development
of man, and (4) progress toward spiritual ideals. These were the
stages through which every knight should pass.

[43] Likeness.

[44] The heroic deeds of King Arthur were pictured in twelve great
colored glass windows.

[45] Mountain and lake.

Where Arthur finds the brand Excalibur.
And also one to the west, and counter to[46] it,
255 And blank: and who shall blazon it? when and how?—
O there, perchance, when all our wars are done,
The brand Excalibur will be cast away.

'So to this hall full quickly rode the King,
In horror lest the work by Merlin wrought,
260 Dreamlike, should on the sudden vanish, wrapt
In unremorseful folds of rolling fire.
And in he rode, and up I glanced, and saw
The golden dragon[47] sparkling over all:
And many of those who burnt the hold, their arms
265 Hack'd, and their foreheads grimed with smoke, and
      sear'd,
Follow'd, and in among bright faces, ours,
Full of the vision, prest: and then the King
Spake to me, being nearest, "Percivale"
(Because the hall was all in tumult—some
270 Vowing, and some protesting), "what is this?"

'O brother, when I told him what had chanced,
My sister's vision, and the rest, his face
Darken'd, as I have seen it more than once,
When some brave deed seem'd to be done in vain,
275 Darken; and "Woe is me, my knights," he cried,
"Had I been here, ye had not sworn the vow."
Bold was mine answer, "Had thyself been here,

---

[46] Opposite.
[47] The symbol of the sovereignty of King Arthur.

ly King, thou wouldst have sworn."   "Yea, yea,"
said he,
Art thou so bold and hast not seen the Grail?"

'"Nay, lord, I heard the sound, I saw the light,   280
ut since I did not see the Holy Thing,
sware a vow to follow it till I saw."

'Then when he ask'd us, knight by knight, if any
lad seen it, all their answers were as one:
Nay, lord, and therefore have we sworn our vows."   285

'"Lo now," said Arthur, "have ye seen a cloud?
What go ye into the wilderness to see?"[48]

'Then Galahad on the sudden, and in a voice
hrilling along the hall to Arthur, call'd,
'But I, Sir Arthur, saw the Holy Grail,   290
saw the Holy Grail and heard a cry—
O Galahad, and O Galahad, follow me.'"

'"Ah, Galahad, Galahad," said the King, "for such
As thou art is the vision, not for these.
Thy holy nun and thou have seen a sign—   295
lolier is none, my Percivale, than she—
A sign to maim this Order which I made.
But ye, that follow but the leader's bell"[49]
Brother, the King was hard upon his knights),

[48] See Matthew XI, 7.
[49] A reference to the flock's following the belled leader, or bell-weather.

300 "Taliessin[50] is our fullest throat of song,
And one hath sung and all the dumb will sing.
Lancelot is Lancelot, and hath overborne
Five knights at once, and every younger knight,
Unproven, holds himself as Lancelot,
305 Till overborne by one, he learns—and ye,
What are ye? Galahads?—no, nor Percivales"
(For thus it pleased the King to range me close
After Sir Galahad); "nay," said he, "but men
With strength and will to right the wrong'd, of powe
310 To lay the sudden heads of violence flat,
Knights that in twelve great battles splash'd and dye
The strong White Horse[51] in his own heathen blood—
But one hath seen, and all the blind will see.
Go, since your vows are sacred, being made:[52]
315 Yet—for ye know the cries of all my realm
Pass thro' this hall—how often, O my knights,
Your places being vacant at my side,
This chance of noble deeds will come and go
Unchallenged, while ye follow wandering fires[53]
320 Lost in the quagmire! Many of you, yea most,
Return no more: ye think I show myself
Too dark a prophet: come now, let us meet
The morrow morn once more in one full field

[50] Taliessin was a Welsh bard of the sixth century A.D. Arthu
hints that knights trying to rival great masters accomplish nothing
While they were good warriors, he hints that they were not yet pre
pared for the higher quest.

[51] The White Horse was the Saxon emblem.

[52] Since they had taken the vow, they must go.

[53] Will-o'-the-wisps, phosphorescent lights often seen over swamp
places.

f gracious pastime, that once more the King
efore ye leave him for this Quest, may count   325
he yet-unbroken strength of all his knights,
ejoicing in that Order which he made."

'So when the sun broke next from under ground,
ll the great table of our Arthur closed
nd clash'd in such a tourney and so full,   330
» many lances broken—never yet
ad Camelot seen the like, since Arthur came;
nd I myself and Galahad, for a strength
'as in us from the vision, overthrew
» many knights that all the people cried,   335
nd almost burst the barriers in their heat,
houting, "Sir Galahad and Sir Percivale!"

'But when the next day brake from under ground—
brother, had you known our Camelot,
uilt by old kings, age after age, so old   340
he King himself had fears that it would fall,
» strange, and rich, and dim; for where the roofs
otter'd toward each other in the sky,
Iet foreheads all along the street of those
Vho watch'd us pass; and lower, and where the long   345
ich galleries, lady-laden, weigh'd the necks
»f dragons clinging to the crazy walls,
'hicker than drops from thunder, showers of flowers
ell as we past; and men and boys astride
»n wyvern, lion, dragon, griffin, swan,[54]   350

[54] Various heraldic devices. The *wyvern* was a winged two-legged
-agon with a serpent's barbed tail. The *griffin* was half eagle and
alf lion.

At all the corners, named us each by name,
Calling "God speed!" but in the ways below
The knights and ladies wept, and rich and poor
Wept, and the King himself could hardly speak
355 For grief, and all in middle street the Queen,
Who rode by Lancelot, wail'd and shriek'd aloud,
"This madness has come on us for our sins."
So to the Gate of the three Queens[55] we came,
Where Arthur's wars are render'd mystically,
360 And thence departed every one his way.

'And I was lifted up in heart, and thought
Of all my late-shown prowess in the lists,
How my strong lance had beaten down the knights,
So many and famous names; and never yet
365 Had heaven appear'd so blue, nor earth so green,
For all my blood danced in me, and I knew
That I should light upon the Holy Grail.

'Thereafter, the dark warning of our King,
That most of us would follow wandering fires,
370 Came like a driving gloom across my mind.
Then every evil word I had spoken once,
And every evil thought I had thought of old,
And every evil deed I ever did,
Awoke and cried, "This Quest is not for thee."
375 And lifting up mine eyes, I found myself
Alone, and in a land of sand and thorns,
And I was thirsty even unto death;
And I, too, cried, "This Quest is not for thee."

[55] See *Gareth and Lynette*, lines 209–231.

'And on I rode, and when I thought my thirst   380
Would slay me, saw deep lawns, and then a brook,
With one sharp rapid, where the crisping [56] white
Play'd ever back upon the sloping wave,
And took both ear and eye; and o'er the brook
Were apple-trees, and apples by the brook
Fallen, and on the lawns. "I will rest here,"   385
I said, "I am not worthy of the Quest";
But even while I drank the brook, and ate
The goodly apples, all these things at once
Fell into dust, and I was left alone,
And thirsting, in a land of sand and thorns. [57]   390

'And then behold a woman at a door
Spinning; and fair the house whereby she sat,
And kind the woman's eyes and innocent,
And all her bearing gracious; and she rose
Opening her arms to meet me, as who should say,   395
"Rest here"; but when I touch'd her, lo! she, too,
Fell into dust and nothing, and the house
Became no better than a broken shed,
And in it a dead babe; and also this
Fell into dust, and I was left alone. [58]   400

'And on I rode, and greater was my thirst.
Then flash'd a yellow gleam across the world,

[56] Rippling or curling.
[57] According to Tennyson the mere gratification of the senses brings no satisfaction.
[58] Love of wife and family were not for Percivale.

And where it smote the plowshare in the field,
The plowman left his plowing, and fell down
405 Before it; where it glitter'd on her pail,
The milkmaid left her milking, and fell down
Before it, and I knew not why, but thought
"The sun is rising," tho' the sun had risen.
Then was I ware of one that on me moved
410 In golden armor with a crown of gold
About a casque all jewels; and his horse
In golden armor jewell'd everywhere:
And on the splendor came, flashing me blind;
And seem'd to me the Lord of all the world,
415 Being so huge. But when I thought he meant
To crush me, moving on me, lo! he, too,
Open'd his arms to embrace me as he came,
And up I went and touch'd him, and he, too,
Fell into dust, and I was left alone
420 And wearying in a land of sand and thorns.[59]

'And I rode on and found a mighty hill,
And on the top, a city wall'd: the spires
Prick'd with incredible pinnacles into heaven.[60]
And by the gateway stirr'd a crowd; and these
425 Cried to me climbing, "Welcome, Percivale!
Thou mightiest and thou purest among men!"
And glad was I and clomb, but found at top
No man, nor any voice. And thence I past
Far thro' a ruinous city, and I saw

[59] Wealth was not to be his portion.
[60] Meaning that the spires were so incredibly high that they seemed
to reach heaven.

That man had once dwelt there; but there I found   430
Only one man of an exceeding age.
'Where is that goodly company," said I,
"That so cried out upon me?" and he had
Scarce any voice to answer, and yet gasp'd,
"Whence and what art thou?" and even as he spoke   435
Fell into dust, and disappear'd, and I
Was left alone once more, and cried in grief,
'Lo, if I find the Holy Grail itself
And touch it, it will crumble into dust."[61]

'And thence I dropt into a lowly vale,[62]   440
Low as the hill was high, and where the vale
Was lowest, found a chapel, and thereby
A holy hermit in a hermitage,
To whom I told my phantoms,[63] and he said:

'"O son, thou hast not true humility,   445
The highest virtue, mother of them all;
For when the Lord of all things made Himself
Naked of glory for His mortal change,
'Take thou my robe,'[64] she said, 'for all is thine,'
And all her form shone forth with sudden light   450
So that the angels were amazed, and she
Follow'd Him down, and like a flying star

[61] Glory and fame do not bring the highest satisfaction, is Tennyson's meaning here.
[62] Valley.
[63] Strange experiences.
[64] Humility.

Led on the gray-hair'd wisdom of the east;[65]
But her thou hast not known: for what is this
455 Thou thoughtest of thy prowess and thy sins?
Thou hast not lost thyself to save thyself
As Galahad." When the hermit made an end,
In silver armor suddenly Galahad shone
Before us, and against the chapel door
460 Laid lance, and enter'd, and we knelt in prayer.
And there the hermit slaked my burning thirst,
And at the sacring of the mass[66] I saw
The holy elements alone; but he,
"Saw ye no more? I, Galahad, saw the Grail,
465 The Holy Grail, descend upon the shrine:
I saw the fiery face as of a child
That smote itself into the bread, and went;
And hither am I come; and never yet
Hath what thy sister taught me first to see,
470 This Holy Thing, fail'd from my side, nor come
Cover'd, but moving with me night and day
Fainter by day, but always in the night
Blood-red, and sliding down the blacken'd marsh
Blood-red, and on the naked mountain top
475 Blood-red, and in the sleeping mere below
Blood-red. And in the strength of this I rode,
Shattering all evil customs everywhere,
And past thro' Pagan[67] realms, and made them mine,
And clash'd with Pagan hordes, and bore them down,

---

[65] The Magi, or wise men of the East, who were guided to Bethlehem by a star at the birth of Jesus. See Matthew II.

[66] The blessing or consecrating of the bread and wine.

[67] Non-Christian.

And broke thro' all, and in the strength of this   480
Come victor. But my time is hard at hand,
And hence I go; and one will crown me king
Far in the spiritual city; and come thou, too,
For thou shalt see the vision when I go."

'While thus he spake, his eye, dwelling on mine,   485
Drew me, with power upon me, till I grew
One with him, to believe as he believed.
Then, when the day began to wane, we went.

'There rose a hill[68] that none but man could climb,
Scarr'd with a hundred wintry watercourses—   490
Storm at the top, and when we gain'd it, storm
Round us and death; for every moment glanced
His silver arms and gloom'd: so quick and thick
The lightnings here and there to left and right
Struck, till the dry old trunks about us, dead,   495
Yea, rotten with a hundred years of death,
Sprang into fire: and at the base we found
On either hand, as far as eye could see,
A great black swamp and of an evil smell,
Part black, part whiten'd with the bones of men,   500
Not to be crost, save that some ancient king
Had built a way, where, link'd with many a bridge,
A thousand piers ran into the great Sea.

[68] Stopford Brooke in *Tennyson: His Art and Relation to Modern Life*, page 327, calls the following passage a "great and lofty vision of the glory of the pure spiritual life" and declares that the picture "is done as no one has done this kind of work since Dante." The "hill" is thought by some to refer to Pisgah, the Mount of Vision. Deut. III, 27.

And Galahad fled along them bridge by bridge,
505 And every bridge as quickly as he crost
Sprang into fire and vanish'd, tho' I yearn'd
To follow; and thrice above him all the heavens
Open'd and blazed[69] with thunder such as seem'd
Shoutings of all the sons of God:[70] and first
510 At once I saw him far on the great Sea,
In silver-shining armor starry-clear;
And o'er his head the Holy Vessel hung
Clothed in white samite or a luminous cloud.
And with exceeding swiftness ran the boat,
515 If boat it were—I saw not whence it came.
And when the heavens open'd and blazed again
Roaring, I saw him like a silver star—
And had he set the sail, or had the boat
Become a living creature clad with wings?
520 And o'er his head the Holy Vessel hung
Redder than any rose, a joy to me,
For now I knew the veil had been withdrawn.
Then in a moment when they blazed again
Opening, I saw the least of little stars
525 Down on the waste, and straight beyond the star
I saw the spiritual city[71] and all her spires
And gateways in a glory like one pearl—
No larger, tho' the goal of all the saints—
Strike from the sea; and from the star there shot
530 A rose-red sparkle to the city, and there
Dwelt, and I knew it was the Holy Grail,

[69] Flashed with lightning and roared with thunder.
[70] See Job XXXVIII, 7—"and all the sons of God shouted for joy."
[71] See Revelation XXI, 10. The New Jerusalem.

Which never eyes on earth again shall see.
Then fell the floods of heaven drowning the deep.
And how my feet recrost the deathful ridge
No memory in me lives; but that I touch'd 535
The chapel-doors at dawn I know; and thence
Taking my war-horse from the holy man,
Glad that no phantom vext[72] me more, return'd
To whence I came, the gate of Arthur's wars.'

'O brother,' ask'd Ambrosius,—'for in sooth 540
These ancient books—and they would win[73] thee—teem,
Only I find not there this Holy Grail,
With miracles and marvels like to these,
Not all unlike; which oftentime I read,
Who read but on my breviary[74] with ease, 545
Till my head swims; and then go forth and pass
Down to the little thorpe[75] that lies so close,
And almost plaster'd like a martin's nest[76]
To these old walls—and mingle with our folk;
And knowing every honest face of theirs 550
As well as ever shepherd knew his sheep,
And every homely secret in their hearts,
Delight myself with gossip and old wives,
And ills and aches, and teethings, lyings-in,
And mirthful sayings, children of the place, 555
That have no meaning half a league away:
Or lulling random squabbles when they rise,

[72] Harassed, or sorely troubled.

[73] Attract.

[74] A condensed book of prayers and services.

[75] Hamlet, small village.

[76] Swallow's nest.

Chafferings[77] and chatterings at the market-cross,[78]
Rejoice, small man,[79] in this small world of mine,
560 Yea, even in their hens and in their eggs—
O brother, saving this Sir Galahad,
Came ye on none but phantoms in your quest,
No man, no woman?'

                                     Then Sir Percivale:
565 'All men, to one so bound by such a vow,
And women were as phantoms. O my brother,
Why wilt thou shame me to confess to thee
How far I falter'd from my quest and vow?
For after I had lain so many nights,
570 A bedmate of the snail and eft[80] and snake,
In grass and burdock, I was changed to wan
And meagre,[81] and the vision had not come;
And then I chanced upon a goodly town
With one great dwelling in the middle of it;
575 Thither I made, and there was I disarm'd
By maidens each as fair as any flower:
But when they led me into hall, behold,
The Princess of that castle was the one,
Brother, and that one only, who had ever
580 Made my heart leap; for when I moved of old
A slender page[82] about her father's hall,

[77] Bargainings.

[78] In medieval times, almost every market place had its cross.
Many of these old crosses still remain.

[79] One living the narrow, or restricted, life of the monastery in
contrast to the wide sweeping spiritual experiences of Sir Galahad.

[80] A small lizard-like animal, or newt.

[81] Pale and thin, or, as we say, "almost a shadow."

[82] Attendant.

And she a slender maiden, all my heart
Went after her with longing: yet we twain
Had never kiss'd a kiss, or vow'd a vow.
And now I came upon her once again,   585
And one had wedded her, and he was dead,
And all his land and wealth and state were hers;
And while I tarried, every day she set
A banquet richer than the day before
By me; for all her longing and her will   590
Was toward me as of old; till one fair morn,
I walking to and fro beside a stream
That flash'd across her orchard underneath
Her castle-walls, she stole upon my walk,
And calling me the greatest of all knights,   595
Embraced me, and so kiss'd me the first time,
And gave herself and all her wealth to me.
Then I remember'd Arthur's warning word,
That most of us would follow wandering fires,
And the Quest faded in my heart. Anon,   600
The heads[83] of all her people drew to me,
With supplication both of knees and tongue:
"We have heard of thee: thou art our greatest knight,
Our Lady says it, and we well believe:
Wed thou our Lady, and rule over us,   605
And thou shalt be as Arthur in our land."
O me, my brother! but one night my vow
Burnt me within, so that I rose and fled,
But wail'd and wept, and hated mine own self,
And ev'n the Holy Quest, and all but her;   610
Then after I was join'd with Galahad

[83] All her leading people.

Cared not for her, nor anything upon earth.'

Then said the monk, 'Poor men, when yule is cold,[84]
Must be content to sit by little fires.
615 And this am I, so that ye care for me
Ever so little; yea, and blest be Heaven
That brought thee here to this poor house of ours
Where all the brethren are so hard to warm
My cold heart with a friend: but O the pity
620 To find thine own first love once more—to hold,
Hold her a wealthy bride within thine arms,
Or all but hold, and then—cast her aside,
Foregoing all her sweetness, like a weed.
For we that want the warmth of double life,
625 We that are plagued with dreams of something sweet
Beyond all sweetness in a life so rich,—
Ah, blessed Lord, I speak too earthly-wise,
Seeing I never stray'd beyond the cell,
But live like an old badger in his earth,
630 With earth about him everywhere, despite
All fast and penance. Saw ye none beside,
None of your knights?'

                              'Yea so,' said Percivale:
'One night my pathway swerving east, I saw
635 The pelican[85] on the casque of our Sir Bors

[84] When Yule is past. Yule means *Christmas*. The Yule-log was
brought in at the Christmas season and a huge fire was kept in the
fire-place then.

[85] According to an old myth, the pelican is a desert-bird that, in
times of scarcity of food for its young, opens its breast and feeds its
brood on its own blood. The pelican on the helmet of Sir Bors was
a symbol of charity.

All in the middle of the rising moon:
And toward him spurr'd, and hail'd him, and he me,
And each made joy of either; then he ask'd,
'Where is he? hast thou seen him—Lancelot?—Once,"   640
Said good Sir Bors, "he dash'd across me—mad,
And maddening what he rode:[86] and when I cried,
'Ridest thou then so hotly on a quest
So holy,' Lancelot shouted, 'Stay me not!
I have been the sluggard, and I ride apace,
For now there is a lion in the way.'[87]   645
So vanish'd."

         'Then Sir Bors had ridden on
Softly, and sorrowing for our Lancelot,
Because his former madness, once the talk
And scandal of our table,[88] had return'd;   650
For Lancelot's kith and kin so worship him
That ill to him is ill to them; to Bors
Beyond the rest: he well had been content
Not to have seen, so Lancelot might have seen,
The Holy Cup of healing; and, indeed,   655
Being so clouded with his grief and love,
Small heart was his after the Holy Quest:
If God would send the vision, well: if not,
The Quest and he were in the hands of Heaven.

'And then, with small adventure met, Sir Bors   660

[86] Spurring his horse to a pitch of frenzied excitement.

[87] Presumably his guilty love for the Queen.

[88] Lancelot had once fallen in love with Queen Elaine, daughter of King Pelles, not the fair Elaine of Astolat. Queen Guinevere, in a jealous fit, had him banished from court. In a fit of madness he wandered two years until restored by the vision of the Holy Grail. See Malory's *Le Morte d'Arthur*, XI, 9, and XII, 4.

Rode to the lonest tract of all the realm,
And found a people there among their crags,
Our race and blood, a remnant that were left
Paynim[89] amid their circles, and the stones
665 They pitch up straight to heaven: and their wise men
Were strong in that old magic which can trace
The wandering of the stars, and scoff'd at him
And this high Quest as at a simple thing:
Told him he follow'd—almost Arthur's words—
670 A mocking fire.[90] "What other fire than he,
Whereby the blood beats, and the blossom blows,
And the sea rolls, and all the world is warm'd?"
And when his answer chafed them, the rough crowd,
Hearing he had a difference with their priests,
675 Seized him, and bound and plunged him into a cell
Of great piled stones; and lying bounded there
In darkness thro' innumerable hours
He heard the hollow-ringing heavens sweep
Over him till by miracle—what else?—
680 Heavy as it was, a great stone slipt and fell,
Such as no wind could move: and thro' the gap
Glimmer'd the streaming scud:[91] then came a night
Still as the day was loud; and thro' the gap
The seven clear stars[92] of Arthur's Table Round—
685 For, brother, so one night, because they roll

[89] Pagans, or non-Christian Britons, or followers of the Druids who worshipped at altars surrounded by circles of long stones stood on end, as at Stonehenge.

[90] These pagans were fire-worshippers and they scoffed at the idea of any other fire than the sun.

[91] "Loose, vapory clouds driven swiftly by the wind."—*Webster*.

[92] The Big Dipper, or the Great Bear.

hro' such a round in heaven, we named the stars,
ejoicing in ourselves and in our King—
nd these, like bright eyes of familiar friends,
 on him shone: "And then to me, to me,"
aid good Sir Bors, "beyond all hopes of mine,   690
Vho scarce had pray'd or ask'd it for myself—
cross the seven clear stars—O grace to me—
 color like the fingers of a hand
efore a burning taper, the sweet Grail
lided and past, and close upon it peal'd   695
 sharp quick thunder." Afterwards, a maid,
Vho kept our holy faith among her kin
n secret, entering, loosed and let him go.'

To whom the monk: 'And I remember now
'hat pelican on the casque: Sir Bors it was   700
Vho spake so low and sadly at our board;
nd mighty reverent at our grace was he:
 square-set man and honest; and his eyes,
n out-door sign of all the warmth within,
miled with his lips—a smile beneath a cloud,   705
3ut Heaven had meant it for a sunny one:
Ay, ay, Sir Bors, who else? But when ye reach'd
The city, found ye all your knights return'd,
Or was there sooth[93] in Arthur's prophecy,
Tell me, and what said each, and what the King?'   710

Then answer'd Percivale: 'And that can I,
Brother, and truly; since the living words
Of so great men as Lancelot and our King

[93] Truth.

Pass not from door to door and out again,
715 But sit within the house. O, when we reach'd
The city, our horses stumbling as they trode
On heaps of ruin,[94] hornless unicorns,[95]
Crack'd basilisks,[96] and splinter'd cockatrices,[97]
And shatter'd talbots,[98] which had left the stones
720 Raw, that they fell from, brought us to the hall.

'And there sat Arthur on the daïs-throne,
And those that had gone out upon the Quest,
Wasted and worn, and but a tithe of them,
And those that had not, stood before the King,
725 Who, when he saw me, rose, and bade me hail,[99]
Saying, "A welfare in thine eye reproves
Our fear of some disastrous chance[100] for thee
On hill, or plain, at sea, or flooding ford.
So fierce a gale made havoc here of late
730 Among the strange devices of our kings;
Yea, shook this newer, stronger hall of ours,
And from the statue Merlin molded for us
Half-wrench'd a golden wing; but now—the Quest,
This vision—hast thou seen the Holy Cup,
735 That Joseph brought of old to Glastonbury?"

[94] Shattered by the fierce gale (line 726).

[95] Fabulous animals, like a horse, but having a single long horn i
the middle of its forehead.

[96] A famous crowned dragon whose look caused instant death.

[97] Fabulous creatures half fowl and half snake, defined by Tennyso
as winged snakes.

[98] Hunting dogs, or mastiffs. All these creatures were represente
in heraldry as symbols of the various knights or groups.

[99] Bade me good health, saluted me.

[100] Mischance.

'So when I told him all thyself hast heard,
Ambrosius, and my fresh but fixt resolve
To pass away into the quiet life,
He answer'd not, but, sharply turning, ask'd
Of Gawain, "Gawain, was this Quest for thee?"   740

'"Nay, lord," said Gawain, "not for such as I.
Therefore I communed with a saintly man,
Who made me sure the Quest was not for me·
For I was much awearied of the Quest:
But found a silk pavilion[101] in a field,   745
And merry maidens in it; and then this gale
Tore my pavilion from the tenting-pin,
And blew my merry maidens all about
With all discomfort; yea, and but for this,
My twelvemonth and a day were pleasant to me."   750

'He ceased; and Arthur turn'd to whom at first
He saw not, for Sir Bors, on entering, push'd
Athwart the throng to Lancelot, caught his hand
Held it, and there, half-hidden by him, stood,
Until the King espied him, saying to him,   755
Hail, Bors! if ever loyal man and true
Could see it, thou hast seen the Grail"; and Bors,
Ask me not, for I may not speak of it:
I saw it"; and the tears were in his eyes.

'Then there remain'd but Lancelot, for the rest   760
Spake but of sundry perils in the storm;

[101] Tent.

Perhaps, like him of Cana in Holy Writ,[102]
Our Arthur kept his best until the last;
"Thou, too, my Lancelot," ask'd the King, "my friend
765 Our mightiest, hath this Quest avail'd for thee?"

"'Our mightiest!" answer'd Lancelot, with a groan,
"O King!"—and when he paused, methought I spied
A dying fire of madness in his eyes—
"O King, my friend, if friend of thine I be,
770 Happier are those that welter in their sin,
Swine in the mud, that cannot see for slime,
Slime of the ditch: but in me lived a sin
So strange, of such a kind, that all of pure,
Noble, and knightly in me twined and clung
775 Round that one sin, until the wholesome flower
And poisonous grew together, each as each,
Not to be pluck'd asunder; and when thy knights
Sware, I sware with them only in the hope
That could I touch or see the Holy Grail
780 They might be pluck'd asunder. Then I spake
To one most holy saint, who wept and said,
That save they could be pluck'd asunder, all
My quest were but in vain; to whom I vow'd
That I would work according as he will'd.
785 And forth I went, and while I yearn'd and strove
To tear the twain asunder in my heart,
My madness came upon me as of old,
And whipt[103] me into waste fields far away;

---

[102] See St. John II, 10. The marriage feast at Cana in Galilee.
[103] Drove.

There was I beaten down by little men,[104]
Mean knights, to whom the moving of my sword   790
And shadow of my spear had been enow[105]
To scare them from me once; and then I came
All in my folly[106] to the naked shore,
Wide flats, where nothing but coarse grasses grew;
But such a blast, my King, began to blow,   795
So loud a blast along the shore and sea,
Ye could not hear the waters for the blast,
Tho' heapt in mounds and ridges all the sea
Drove like a cataract, and all the sand
Swept like a river, and the clouded heavens   800
Were shaken with the motion and the sound.
And blackening in the sea-foam sway'd a boat,
Half-swallow'd in it, anchor'd with a chain;
And in my madness to myself I said,
'I will embark and I will lose myself,   805
And in the great sea wash away my sin.'
I burst the chain, I sprang into the boat.
Seven days I drove along the dreary deep,
And with me drove the moon and all the stars;
And the wind fell, and on the seventh night   810
I heard the shingle[107] grinding in the surge,
And felt the boat shock earth,[108] and looking up
Behold, the enchanted towers of Carbonek,[109]

[104] Men of less strength and courage.
[105] Enough.
[106] Madness.
[107] Coarse gravel and small stones.
[108] Touch the shore.
[109] A castle which for a time sheltered the Holy Grail. King Pelles
was said to have lived there and guarded the Grail.

A castle like a rock upon a rock,
815 With chasm-like portals open to the sea,
And steps that met the breaker! there was none
Stood near it but a lion on each side
That kept the entry, and the moon was full.
Then from the boat I leapt, and up the stairs.
820 There drew my sword. With sudden-flaring manes
Those two great beasts rose upright like a man,
Each gript a shoulder, and I stood between;
And, when I would have smitten them, heard a voice.
'Doubt not, go forward; if thou doubt, the beasts
825 Will tear thee piecemeal.' Then with violence
The sword was dash'd from out my hand, and fell.
And up into the sounding hall I past;
But nothing in the sounding hall I saw,
No bench nor table, painting on the wall
830 Or shield of knight; only the rounded moon
Thro' the tall oriel[110] on the rolling sea.
But always in the quiet house I heard,
Clear as a lark, high o'er me as a lark,
A sweet voice singing in the topmost tower
835 To the eastward: up I climb'd a thousand steps
With pain: as in a dream I seem'd to climb
For ever: at the last I reach'd a door,
A light was in the crannies, and I heard,
'Glory and joy and honor to our Lord
840 And to the Holy Vessel of the Grail.'
Then in my madness I essay'd the door;
It gave,[111] and thro' a stormy glare, a heat

[110] A kind of bay window.
[111] Opened.

s from a seventimes-heated furnace,[112] I,
Blasted and burnt, and blinded as I was,
With such a fierceness that I swoon'd away—   845
, yet methought I saw the Holy Grail,
All pall'd[113] in crimson samite, and around
Great angels, awful shapes, and wings and eyes.
And but for all my madness and my sin,
And then my swooning, I had sworn I saw   850
That which I saw; but what I saw was veil'd
And cover'd; and this Quest was not for me."

'So speaking, and here ceasing, Lancelot left
The hall long silent, till Sir Gawain—nay,
Brother, I need not tell thee foolish words —   855
A reckless and irreverent knight was he,
Now bolden'd by the silence of his King,—
Well, I will tell thee: "O King, my liege," he said,
Hath Gawain fail'd in any quest of thine?
When have I stinted stroke in foughten field?   860
But as for thine, my good friend Percivale,
Thy holy nun and thou have driven men mad,
Yea, made our mightiest madder than our least.
But by mine eyes and by mine ears I swear,
I will be deafer than the blue-eyed cat,[114]   865
And thrice as blind as any noonday owl,
To holy virgins in their ecstasies,
Henceforward."

[112] See Daniel III, 19.
[113] Covered.
[114] White cats with blue eyes were generally deaf.

'"Deafer," said the blameless King,
870 "Gawain, and blinder unto holy things
Hope not to make thyself by idle vows,
Being too blind to have desire to see.
But if indeed there came a sign from heaven,
Blessed are Bors, Lancelot, and Percivale,
875 For these have seen according to their sight.[115]
For every fiery prophet in old times,
And all the sacred madness of the bard,
When God made music thro' them, could but speak
His music by the framework and the chord;
880 And as ye saw it ye have spoken truth.

'"Nay—but thou errest, Lancelot: never yet
Could all of true and noble in knight and man
Twine round one sin, whatever it might be,
With such a closeness, but apart there grew,
885 Save that he were the swine thou spakest of,
Some root of knighthood and pure nobleness;
Whereto see thou, that it may bear its flower.

'"And spake I not too truly, O my knights?
Was I too dark a prophet when I said
890 To those who went upon the Holy Quest,
That most of them would follow wandering fires,
Lost in the quagmire?—lost to me and gone,
And left me gazing at a barren bard,
And a lean Order—scarce return'd a tithe—

[115] The five persons who had seen the Grail were: the nun,
Galahad, Sir Percivale, Sir Lancelot, and Sir Bors. Each had se
it in the light of his own nature and experience.

nd out of those to whom the vision came   895
Iy greatest[116] hardly will believe he saw;
.nother[117] hath beheld it afar off,
.nd leaving human wrongs to right themselves,
'ares but to pass into the silent life.
.nd one[118] hath had the vision face to face,   900
nd now his chair desires him here in vain,
Iowever they may crown him otherwhere.

'"And some among you held, that if the King
Iad seen the sight he would have sworn the vow:
Iot easily, seeing that the King must guard   905
'hat which he rules, and is but as the hind[119]
'o whom a space of land is given to plow.
Vho may not wander from the allotted field
efore his work be done; but, being done,
et visions of the night or of the day   910
ome, as they will; and many a time they come,
Intil this earth he walks on seems not earth,
'his light that strikes his eyeball is not light,
'his air that smites his forehead is not air
ut vision[120]—yea, his very hand and foot—   915

[116] Lancelot.
[117] Percivale.
[118] Galahad.
[119] Peasant.
[120] Tennyson, in commenting on the Holy Grail, says, "I have ex-
·essed there my strong feeling of the Reality of the Unseen. The
id, where the King speaks of his work and of his visions, is intended
· be the summing up of all in the highest note by the highest of
uman men. These three lines in Arthur's speech (lines 911–13) are
piritually) the central lines of the Idylls."

In moments when he feels he cannot die,
And knows himself no vision to himself,
Nor the high God a vision, nor that One
Who rose again: ye have seen what ye have seen."

920 'So spake the King: I knew not all he meant.'

THE PASSING OF ARTHUR

HAT story which the bold Sir Bedivere,[1]
First made and latest left of all the knights,
Told, when the man was no more than a voice
In the white winter of his age, to those
With whom he dwelt, new faces, other minds.   5

For on their march to westward,[2] Bedivere,
Who slowly paced among the slumbering host,
Heard in his tent the moanings of the King:[3]

'I found Him in the shining of the stars,
I mark'd Him in the flowering of His fields,   10
But in His ways with men I find Him not.
I waged His wars, and now I pass and die.
O me! for why is all around us here
As if some lesser god had made the world,
But had not force to shape it as he would,   15
Till the High God behold it from beyond,
And enter it, and make it beautiful?
Or else as if the world were wholly fair,
But that these eyes of men are dense and dim,

[1] Sir Bedivere (bĕd′ĭ-vēr) was knighted at the coronation of the
King and was called by some the King's cup-bearer.
[2] The King has just returned from his war with Lancelot in Brittany,
and is now going westward to meet the traitor Modred at the head of
rebel host.
[3] Near the end of his long career.

20 And have not power to see it as it is:
Perchance, because we see not to the close;—
For I, being simple, thought to work His will,
And have but stricken with the sword in vain;
And all whereon I lean'd in wife and friend
25 Is traitor to my peace, and all my realm
Reels back into the beast,[4] and is no more.
My God, thou hast forgotten me in my death:
Nay — God my Christ — I pass[5] but shall not die.'

Then, ere that last weird battle in the west,
30 There came on Arthur sleeping, Gawain kill'd
In Lancelot's war, the ghost of Gawain blown
Along a wandering wind, and past his ear
Went shrilling,[6] 'Hollow, hollow all delight!
Hail, King! to-morrow thou shalt pass away.
35 Farewell! there is an isle of rest for thee.
And I am blown along a wandering wind,
And hollow, hollow, hollow all delight.'
And fainter onward, like wild birds that change
Their season[7] in the night and wail their way
40 From cloud to cloud, down the long wind the dream
Shrill'd; but in going mingled with dim cries
Far in the moonlit haze among the hills,
As of some lonely city sack'd by night,
When all is lost, and wife and child with wail[8]

[4] Returns to a condition of wild and savage disorder.
[5] Here *pass* is used in the sense of *depart*.
[6] Crying in shrill tones.
[7] Go on long flights, or migrate to avoid severe winters.
[8] With cries of wailing for lost ones.

ass to new lords; and Arthur woke and call'd,   45
Who spake? A dream. O light upon the wind,
'hine, Gawain, was the voice — are these dim cries
'hine? or doth all that haunts the waste and wild
Iourn, knowing it will go along with me?'

   This heard the bold Sir Bedivere and spake: 50
) me, my King, let pass whatever will,
lves,[9] and the harmless glamour of the field;
ut in their stead thy name and glory cling
o all high places like a golden cloud
or ever: but as yet thou shalt not pass.   55
ight was Gawain in life, and light in death
Gawain, for the ghost is as the man;
nd care not thou for dreams from him, but rise —
hear the steps of Modred in the west,
nd with him many of thy people, and knights   60
nce thine, whom thou hast loved, but grosser grown
han heathen, spitting at[10] their vows and thee.
ight well in heart they know thee for the King.
rise, go forth and conquer as of old.'

   Then spake King Arthur to Sir Bedivere: 65
'ar other is this battle in the west
'hereto we move, than when we strove in youth,
nd brake the petty kings, and fought with Rome,
r thrust the heathen from the Roman wall,[11]

[9] Fairies.
[10] Scorning and breaking.
[11] The Roman wall was built across the island from the Solway to
e Tyne to keep out the Picts and Scots.

70 And shook him thro' the north. Ill doom is mine[12]
   To war against my people and my knights.
   The king who fights his people fights himself.
   And they my knights, who loved me once, the stroke
   That strikes them dead is as my death to me.
75 Yet let us hence, and find or feel a way
   Thro' this blind haze, which ever since I saw
   One[13] lying in the dust at Almesbury,
   Hath folded in the passes of the world.'[14]

   Then rose the King and moved his host by night,
80 And ever push'd Sir Modred, league by league,
   Back to the sunset bound of Lyonesse —
   A land of old upheaven[15] from the abyss
   By fire, to sink into the abyss again;
   Where fragments of forgotten peoples dwelt,
85 And the long mountains ended in a coast
   Of ever-shifting sand, and far away
   The phantom circle[16] of a moaning sea.
   There the pursuer could pursue no more,
   And he that fled no further fly the King;
90 And there, that day when the great light of heaven
   Burn'd at his lowest[17] in the rolling year,
   On the waste sand by the waste sea they closed.
   Nor even yet had Arthur fought a fight

   [12] Sad misfortune.
   [13] Queen Guinevere.
   [14] Clouded the roadways.
   [15] Upheaved by volcanic action.
   [16] The far horizon.
   [17] The shortest day in winter, December 21.

Like this last, him, weird battle of the west.
A deathwhite mist slept over sand and sea: 95
Whereof the chill, to him who breathed it, drew
Down with his blood, till all his heart was cold
With formless fear; and ev'n on Arthur fell
Confusion, since he saw not whom he fought.
For friend and foe were shadows in the mist,   100
And friend slew friend not knowing whom he slew;
And some had visions out of golden youth,
And some beheld the faces of old ghosts
Look in upon the battle; and in the mist
Was many a noble deed, many a base,   105
And chance and craft and strength in single fights,
And ever and anon with host to host
Shocks, and the splintering spear, the hard mail [18]
       hewn,
Shield-breakings, and the clash of brands, the crash
Of battleaxes on shatter'd helms, and shrieks   110
After the Christ, of those who falling down
Look'd up for heaven, and only saw the mist;
And shouts of heathen and the traitor knights,
Oaths, insult, filth, and monstrous blasphemies,
Sweat, writhings, anguish, labouring of the lungs   115
In that close mist, and cryings for the light,
Moans of the dying, and voices of the dead.

  Last, as by some one deathbed after wail
Of suffering, silence follows, or thro' death
Or deathlike swoon, thus over all that shore,   120
Save for some whisper of the seething seas,

[18] Coat of mail, or armor.

A dead hush fell; but when the dolorous[19] day
Grew drearier toward twilight falling, came
A bitter wind, clear from the North, and blew
125 The mist aside, and with that wind the tide
Rose, and the pale King glanced across the field
Of battle: but no man was moving there;
Nor any cry of Christian heard thereon,
Nor yet of heathen; only the wan wave
130 Brake in among dead faces, to and fro
Swaying the helpless hands, and up and down
Tumbling the hollow helmets of the fallen,
And shiver'd brands that once had fought with Rome,
And rolling far along the gloomy shores
135 The voice of days of old and days to be.[20]

Then spake King Arthur to Sir Bedivere,
And whiter than the mist that all day long
Had held the field of battle was the King:

'Hearest thou this great voice that shakes the world,
140 And wastes the narrow realm whereon we move,
And beats upon the faces of the dead,
My dead, as tho' they had not died for me?—
O Bedivere, for on my heart hath fall'n
Confusion, till I know not what I am,
145 Nor whence I am, nor whether I be King,
Behold, I seem but King among the dead.'

[19] Grievous, or bitterly sad.
[20] Noise of wind and wave seemed like the voices of heroes of other days.

Then spake the bold Sir Bedivere: 'My King,
ing everywhere! and so the dead have kings,
here also will I worship thee as King.
et still thy life is whole, and still I live   150
Vho love thee; but who hates thee, he that brought
he heathen back among us, yonder stands,
Iodred unharm'd, the traitor of thine house.' [21]

Then spake the King: 'My house hath been my
          doom.
ut call not thou this traitor of my house   155
Vho hath but dwelt beneath one roof with me.
Iy house are rather they who sware my vows,
ea, even while they brake them, own'd me King.
nd well for thee, saying in my dark hour,
Vhen all the purport of my throne[22] hath fail'd,   160
hat quick[23] or dead thou holdest me for King.
ing am I, whatsoever be their cry;
nd one last act of knighthood shalt thou see
et, ere I pass.'   And uttering this the King
Iade at the man: then Modred smote his liege[24]   165
Iard on that helm which many a heathen sword
Iad beaten thin; while Arthur at one blow,
triking the last stroke with Excalibur,
lew him, and all but slain himself, he fell.

So all day long the noise of battle roll'd   170

[21] Household, or Knights of the Round Table.
[22] Aim of my reign.
[23] Living.
[24] Lord.

Among the mountains by the winter sea;
Until King Arthur's Table, man by man,
Had fall'n in Lyonesse about their lord,
King Arthur. Then, because his wound was deep,
175 The bold Sir Bedivere uplifted him,
And bore him to a chapel nigh the field,
A broken chancel[25] with a broken cross,
That stood on a dark strait[26] of barren land:
On one side lay the Ocean, and on one
180 Lay a great water,[27] and the moon was full.

Then spake King Arthur to Sir Bedivere:
'The sequel[28] of to-day unsolders[29] all
The goodliest fellowship of famous knights
Whereof this world holds record. Such a sleep
185 They sleep — the men I loved. I think that we
Shall never more, at any future time,
Delight our souls with talk of knightly deeds,
Walking about the gardens and the halls
Of Camelot, as in the days that were.
190 I perish by this people which I made,—
Tho' Merlin sware that I should come again
To rule once more; but, let what will be, be,
I am so deeply smitten thro' the helm
That without help I cannot last till morn.
195 Thou therefore take my brand Excalibur,[30]

[25] The part of the chapel where the altar stands.
[26] A dark narrow neck or strip.
[27] A lake.
[28] The results of to-day's battle.
[29] Breaks the ties of fellowship, because of the numbers slain.
[30] The sword, Excalibur, given him by the Lady of the Lake.

Which was my pride: for thou rememberest how
In those old days, one summer noon, an arm
Rose up from out the bosom of the lake,
Clothed in white samite, mystic, wonderful,
Holding the sword — and how I row'd across   200
And took it, and have worn it, like a king;
And, wheresoever I am sung or told
In aftertime, this also shall be known:
But now delay not: take Excalibur,
And fling him far into the middle mere: 205
Watch what thou seëst, and lightly[31] bring me word.'

　To him replied the bold Sir Bedivere:
'It is not meet, Sir King, to leave thee thus,
Aidless, alone, and smitten thro' the helm —
A little thing may harm a wounded man;   210
Yet I thy hest[32] will all perform at full,
Watch what I seëst, and lightly bring thee word.'

　So saying, from the ruin'd shrine he stept,
And in the moon athwart the place of tombs,
Where lay the mighty bones of ancient men,   215
Old knights, and over them the sea-wind sang
Shrill, chill, with flakes of foam. He, stepping down
By zigzag paths, and juts of pointed rock,
Came on the shining levels of the lake.

　There drew he forth the brand Excalibur,   220
And o'er him, drawing it, the winter moon,

[31] Immediately, quickly.
[32] Behest, or command.

Brightening the skirts of a long cloud, ran forth
And sparkled keen with frost against the hilt.[33]
For all the haft twinkled with diamond sparks,
225 Myriads of topaz-lights, and jacinth-work
Of subtlest jewellery. He gazed so long
That both his eyes were dazzled as he stood,
This way and that dividing the swift mind,
In act to throw: but at the last it seem'd
230 Better to leave Excalibur conceal'd
There in the many-knotted waterflags,
That whistled stiff and dry about the marge.
So strode he back slow to the wounded King.

Then spake King Arthur to Sir Bedivere:
235 'Hast thou perform'd my mission which I gave?
What is it thou hast seen? or what hast heard?'

And answer made the bold Sir Bedivere:
'I heard the ripple washing in the reeds,
And the wild water lapping on the crag.'

240   To whom replied King Arthur, faint and pale:
'Thou hast betray'd thy nature and thy name,
Not rendering true answer, as beseem'd[34]
Thy fëalty,[35] nor like a noble knight:
For surer sign had follow'd, either hand,
245 Or voice, or else a motion of the mere.
This is a shameful thing for men to lie.

[33] Sword-handle, same as *haft* in the next line.
[34] Became, or fitted well.
[35] Your loyalty to your King.

Yet now, I charge thee, quickly go again,
As thou art lief[36] and dear, and do the thing
I bade thee, watch, and lightly bring me word.'

Then went Sir Bedivere the second time   250
Across the ridge, and paced beside the mere,
Counting the dewy pebbles, fix'd in thought;
But when he saw the wonder of the hilt,
How curiously and strangely chased,[37] he smote
His palms together, and he cried aloud: 255

'And if indeed I cast the brand away,
Surely a precious thing, one worthy note,
Should thus be lost for ever from the earth,
Which might have pleased the eyes of many men.
What good should follow this, if this were done?   260
What harm, undone? Deep harm to disobey,
Seeing obedience is the bond of rule.
Were it well to obey then, if a king demand
An act unprofitable, against himself?
The King is sick, and knows not what he does.   265
What record, or what relic of my lord
Should be to aftertime, but empty breath
And rumours of a doubt? But were this kept,
Stored in some treasure-house of mighty kings,
Some one might show it at a joust of arms,   270
Saying, "King Arthur's sword, Excalibur,
Wrought by the lonely maiden of the Lake.
Nine years she wrought it, sitting in the deeps

[36] Greatly beloved.
[37] Wondrously engraved.

Upon the hidden bases of the hills."
275 So might some old man speak in the aftertime
To all the people, winning reverence.
But now much honour and much fame were lost.'

So spake he, clouded with his own conceit,[38]
And hid Excalibur the second time,
280 And so strode back slow to the wounded King.

Then spoke King Arthur, breathing heavily:
'What is it thou hast seen? or what hast heard?'

And answer made the bold Sir Bedivere:
'I heard the water lapping on the crag,
285 And the long ripple washing in the reeds.'

To whom replied King Arthur, much in wrath:
'Ah, miserable and unkind, untrue,
Unknightly, traitor-hearted! Woe is me!
Authority forgets[39] a dying king,
290 Laid widow'd of[40] the power in his eye
That bow'd the will. I see thee what thou art,
For thou, the latest-left of all my knights,
In whom should meet the offices of all,
Thou wouldst betray me for the precious hilt;
295 Either from lust of gold, or like a girl
Valuing the giddy pleasure of the eyes.
Yet, for [41] a man may fail in duty twice,

[38] His own false notion.
[39] Deserts.
[40] Deprived of.
[41] Since.

And the third time may prosper, get thee hence:
But, if thou spare to fling Excalibur,
I will arise and slay thee with my hands.' 300

    Then quickly rose Sir Bedivere, and ran,
And, leaping down the ridges lightly, plunged
Among the bulrush beds, and clutch'd the sword,
And strongly wheel'd[42] and threw it. The great brand
Made lightnings in the splendour of the moon, 305
And flashing round and round, and whirl'd in an arch,
Shot like a streamer of the northern morn,[43]
Seen where the moving isles[44] of winter shock
By night, with noises of the Northern Sea.
So flash'd and fell the brand Excalibur: 310
But ere he dipt[45] the surface, rose an arm
Clothed in white samite, mystic, wonderful,
And caught him[46] by the hilt, and brandish'd him
Three times, and drew him under in the mere.
And lightly went the other to the King. 315

    Then spoke King Arthur, drawing thicker breath:
'Now see I by thine eyes that this is done.
Speak out: what is it thou hast heard, or seen?'

    And answer made the bold Sir Bedivere:
'Sir King, I closed mine eyelids, lest the gems 320

[42] Whirled the sword.
[43] The Aurora Borealis, or Northern Lights.
[44] Moving icebergs.
[45] Reached, or touched.
[46] It.

Should blind my purpose, for I never saw,
Nor shall see, here or elsewhere, till I die,
Not tho' I live three lives of mortal men,
So great a miracle as yonder hilt.
325 Then with both hands I flung him, wheeling him;
But when I look'd again, behold an arm,
Clothed in white samite, mystic, wonderful,
That caught him by the hilt, and brandish'd him
Three times, and drew him under in the mere.'

330 And answer made King Arthur, breathing hard:
'My end draws nigh; 'tis time that I were gone.
Make broad thy shoulders to receive my weight,
And bear me to the margin; yet I fear
My wound hath taken cold, and I shall die.'

335 So saying, from the pavement[47] he half rose,
Slowly, with pain, reclining on his arm,
And looking wistfully with wide blue eyes
As in a picture. Him Sir Bedivere
Remorsefully regarded thro' his tears,
340 And would have spoken, but he found not words;
Then took with care, and kneeling on one knee,
O'er both his shoulders drew the languid hands,
And rising bore him thro' the place of tombs.

But, as he walk'd, King Arthur panted hard,
345 Like one that feels a nightmare on his bed
When all the house is mute. So sigh'd the King,
Muttering and murmuring at his ear, 'Quick, quick!

[47] Floor.

I fear it is too late, and I shall die.'
But the other swiftly strode from ridge to ridge,
Clothed with his breath,[48] and looking, as he walk'd,   350
Larger than human on the frozen hills.
He heard the deep behind him, and a cry
Before. His own thought drove him like a goad.
Dry clash'd his harness in the icy caves
And barren chasms, and all to left and right   355
The bare black cliff clang'd round him, as he based[49]
His feet on juts[50] of slippery crag that rang
Sharp-smitten with the dint of armed heels —
And on a sudden, lo! the level lake,
And the long glories of the winter moon.   360

    Then saw they how there hove[51] a dusky barge,
Dark as a funeral scarf from stem to stern,
Beneath them; and descending they were ware[52]
That all the decks were dense[53] with stately forms,
Black-stoled,[54] black-hooded, like a dream — by these   365
Three Queens[55] with crowns of gold: and from them rose
A cry that shiver'd to the tingling stars,
And, as it were one voice, an agony

[48] Surrounded by frost-vapors from his breath.
[49] Firmly fixed.
[50] Outcroppings, or projections.
[51] Came into view.
[52] Aware.
[53] Filled, or crowded.
[54] Black gowned.
[55] Faith, Hope, Love. Tennyson's symbolical interpretation of Malory's Queen Morgan le Fay, Arthur's sister; Queen of Northgates; and Queen of the Waste Lands.—*Malory, Morte d'Arthur, xxi, 6*.

Of lamentation, like a wind that shrills
370 All night in a waste land, where no one comes,
Or hath come, since the making of the world.

Then murmur'd Arthur, 'Place me in the barge.'
So to the barge they came.   There those three Queens
Put forth their hands, and took the King, and wept.
375 But she, that rose the tallest[56] of them all
And fairest, laid his head upon her lap,
And loosed the shatter'd casque,[57] and chafed his hands,
And call'd him by his name, complaining loud,
And dropping bitter tears against a brow
380 Striped with dark blood: for all his face was white
And colourless, and like the wither'd moon
Smote by the fresh beam of the springing east;
And all his greaves[58] and cuisses[59] dash'd with drops
Of onset;[60] and the light and lustrous curls—
385 That made his forehead like a rising sun
High from the daïs-throne[61]— were parch'd with dust;
Or clotted into points and hanging loose,
Mix'd with the knightly growth that fringed his lips.
So like a shatter'd column lay the King;
390 Not like that Arthur who, with lance in rest,
From spur to plume a star of tournament,
Shot thro' the lists at Camelot, and charged
Before the eyes of ladies and of kings.

[56] Love.
[57] Shattered helmet.
[58] A piece of the armor that protected the lower leg.
[59] Thigh armor.
[60] Battle-blood.
[61] Throne under a canopy.

Then loudly cried the bold Sir Bedivere:
'Ah! my Lord Arthur, whither shall I go?   395
Where shall I hide my forehead and my eyes?
For now I see the true old times are dead,
When every morning brought a noble chance,[62]
And every chance brought out a noble knight.
Such times have been not since the light that led   400
The holy Elders[63] with the gift of myrrh.
But now the whole Round Table is dissolved
Which was an image of the mighty world,
And I, the last, go forth companionless,
And the days darken round me, and the years,   405
Among new men, strange faces, other minds.'

And slowly answer'd Arthur from the barge:
'The old order changeth, yielding place to new,
And God fulfils himself in many ways,
Lest one good custom should corrupt the world.   410
Comfort thyself: what comfort is in me?
I have lived my life, and that which I have done
May He within himself make pure! but thou,
If thou shouldst never see my face again,
Pray for my soul. (More things are wrought by prayer   415
Than this world dreams of.[64] Wherefore, let thy voice
Rise like a fountain for me night and day.
For what are men better than sheep or goats
That nourish a blind life[65] within the brain,

[62] A big opportunity.

[63] The three Wise Men who followed the star that shone above
Bethlehem's manger.

[64] Tennyson was a firm believer in the power of prayer.

[65] An unconscious life.

420 If, knowing God, they lift not hands of prayer[66]
Both for themselves and those who call them friend?
For so the whole round earth is every way
· Bound by gold chains about the feet of God.
But now farewell. I am going a long way
425 With these thou seest — if indeed I go
(For all my mind is clouded with a doubt)—
To the island-valley of Avilion;[67]
Where falls not hail, or rain, or any snow.
Nor ever wind blows loudly; but it lies
430 Deep-meadow'd, happy, fair with orchard lawns
And bowery hollows crown'd with summer sea,
Where I will heal me of my grievous wound.'

So said he, and the barge with oar and sail
Moved from the brink, like some full-breasted swan
435 That, fluting a wild carol ere her death,
Ruffles her pure cold plume,[68] and takes the flood
With swarthy webs.[69] Long stood Sir Bedivere
Revolving[70] many memories, till the hull[71]
Look'd one black dot against the verge of dawn,[72]
440 And on the mere the wailing died away.

But when that moan had past for ever more,
The stillness of the dead world's winter dawn

[66] In prayer, the ancients stood with hands upraised.
[67] The earthly heaven of the Britains.
[68] Raises her wings.
[69] And swims with black web-feet.
[70] Thinking of.
[71] The barge's body.
[72] Looked like a black dot as it went eastward against the eastern sunrise light.

Amazed him, and he groan'd, 'The King is gone.'
And therewithal came on him the weird rhyme,
'From the great deep to the great deep he goes.'   445

Whereat he slowly turn'd and slowly clomb[73]
The last hard footstep of that iron crag;
Thence mark'd[74] the black hull moving yet, and cried,
'He passes to be King among the dead,
And after healing of his grievous wound   450
He comes again; but — if he come no more —
O me, be yon dark Queens in yon black boat,
Who shriek'd and wail'd, the three whereat we gazed
On that high day, when, clothed with living light,
They stood before his throne in silence, friends   455
Of Arthur, who should help him at his need?'

Then from the dawn it seem'd there came, but faint
As from beyond the limit of the world,
Like the last echo born of a great cry,
Sounds, as if some fair city were one voice   460
Around a king returning from his wars.

Thereat once more he moved about, and clomb
Ev'n to the highest he could climb, and saw,
Straining his eyes beneath an arch of hand,
Or thought he saw, the speck that bare the King,   465
Down that long water opening on the deep
Somewhere far off, pass on and on, and go
From less to less and vanish into light.
And the new sun rose bringing the new year.

[73] Climbed.
[74] Saw.

QUESTIONS FOR CLASS STUDY

IDYLLS OF THE KING

GENERAL QUESTIONS

1. Tell briefly how Tennyson came to write Idylls of the King.

2. What are the leading sources of the story of King Arthur?

3. Explain van Dyke's meaning when he says that the story of the Idylls is "a parable of the life of man."

4. Summarize very briefly each of the twelve stories in the completed poem.

5. Give a more detailed summary of the story of Gareth and Lynette.

6. Tell more fully the story of Lancelot and Elaine.

7. Give a summary of The Passing of Arthur. What is meant by "sense at war with soul"?

8. Look up and report something of the condition of affairs in other countries during the days of King Arthur.

9. What period was this in the world's history? Tell some of the chief characteristics of the period.

10. What seem to you the best reasons for reading and studying these poems?

THE COMING OF ARTHUR

1. What was the condition of Leodogran's kingdom?
2. Who were "the heathen host"?

3. Explain "the beast was ever more and more, bu man was less and less."

4. Why is the fact given in the first four lines s important?

5. Cite passages showing the extent to which th kingdom of Leodogran was overrun.

6. To whom did Leodogran appeal for help?

ARTHUR HEEDS CALL OF LEODOGRAN

7. Explain the meaning of line 46.

8. What was the symbol of Arthur's kinglihood?

9. Why did he now ride "a simple knight among hi knights"?

10. Explain why Guinevere failed to recogniz Arthur.

11. What tells of the effect of the sight of Guinever on Arthur?

12. What great deeds did he first perform?

13. What doubts "smoulder'd" in the hearts of th great Lords and Barons of the realm?

14. Why was the matter of his birth so important

15. What dream did Arthur now entertain fo Guinevere?

16. Cite passages showing the appearance o Guinevere.

17. What effect did the new ambition of Arthur hav on his prowess in battle?

18. Describe briefly the battle with the kings.

19. Explain "So like a painted battle the war stoo silenced."

20. Why was joy now lord in the heart of Arthur?

21. Who was the warrior "whom he loved and hon-ored most"?

22. Explain the meaning of "each had warded ither in the fight."

23. What mutual pledge did Arthur and his loved night make?

24. Explain "Man's word is God in man."

ARTHUR CLAIMS GUINEVERE AS REWARD

25. What request did he now make of King Leodo-ran?

26. Why did Leodogran hesitate to comply with the equest?

27. What did the king's chamberlain tell of Arthur's irth?

28. Who was Merlin and what was his place in rthur's kingdom?

29. Who was Bleys and what was his work?

30. Explain the meaning of the king's answer to the hamberlain.

31. What question did Leodogran now put to King rthur's messengers?

32. What in brief was Bedivere's answer?

33. What relationship between Bellicent and Arthur revealed in the answer?

34. Why should Merlin keep secret the birth of rthur? Cite the passages proving your answer.

35. What in this answer is shown of the power and aft of Merlin?

36. What effect did this answer have on King Leodogran?

BELLICENT COMES TO COURT

37. What question did Leodogran ask Bellicent at the feast?

38. What was her answer?

39. Cite passages from her answer showing the character and nature of King Arthur.

40. Describe Arthur's court as pictured in her answer.

41. Tell the story of how King Arthur secured his sword.

42. Explain the meaning of the legends on the blade.

43. Why was Arthur sad when he saw the second legend?

44. What assurance did Merlin give him?

45. What further question did the king ask of Bellicent?

46. Why were the sons, Gawain and Modred, sent from the chamber?

47. What is told us of Modred in "laid his ear beside the doors, and there half-heard"?

48. What in brief is Bellicent's explanation of Arthur's birth?

49. What characteristics of Arthur in childhood are revealed in Bellicent's answer?

50. Why had Bellicent been summoned to Bleys on his deathbed?

51. What light did Bleys' deathbed tale throw upon the birth of Arthur?

52. Why did Merlin answer her in "riddling triplets"? Explain.

53. What, if any, light did these triplets throw on Arthur's birth?

54. What final counsel did Bellicent give Leodogran?

55. Cite the passage showing further efforts he made to arrive at a conclusion.

56. What caused him finally to send a favorable answer to Arthur?

The Marriage of King Arthur

57. Why did Arthur trust Lancelot with the responsibility of bringing the queen?

58. Tell briefly the story of the marriage.

59. What mutual vow did they take?

60. What final blessing did the holy Dubric pronounce?

61. What hints concerning Arthur's kingdom are given in the trumpet song?

62. What answer did Arthur make to the lords from Rome who now claimed tribute as of yore?

63. What tells of Arthur's skill to unify his kingdom?

64. What tells of his prowess in battle?

65. Give a brief summary of the story of *The Coming of Arthur*.

Gareth and Lynette

1. Who were the other sons of Bellicent?

2. What, in lines 5–32, tells of the character of Gareth?

3. What resolution did he make?

4. What was his one ambition?

5. What do Gareth's words (lines 25–32) tell of his brothers?

GARETH AND HIS INDULGENT MOTHER

6. What is the relation between Gareth and his mother?

7. What is the point of Gareth's story of the lusty youth and the eagle's egg?

8. What reasons does Bellicent first give for not releasing Gareth to Arthur's hall? Point out vivid descriptive words and phrases in her words (lines 72–97).

9. What kind of man was Gareth's father?

10. What does Bellicent offer her son as a substitute for Arthur's wars?

11. Explain in your own words the meaning of Gareth's story (lines 98–118).

12. What in these passages shows the true character of Gareth?

13. How does Bellicent (lines 119–129) contradict herself? Explain.

14. Explain fully Gareth's answer.

15. What is shown of Gareth by his reply, "a hard one, or a hundred, so I go" (line 146)?

16. What is Bellicent's purpose in asking a proof of Gareth?

GARETH WELCOMES A SEVERE TEST

17. What proof did she require?

18. Why does Gareth welcome so severe a proof?

19. Why does he choose so early an hour for departure?

20. What tells how the attendants felt as they approached Camelot?

21. Describe in your own words the gate of Camelot. What fine words and phrases did Tennyson use in his description (lines 209–231)?

22. What in brief did the old seer at the gate tell Gareth?

23. Explain the seer's statement (lines 286–287) "thou goest up to mock the king."

24. How does Gareth look upon the *one white lie* he has told?

25. Why was the sound of the clashing of arms good to Gareth's ears?

26. Why was "his young heart hammering in his ears"?

27. Why does Gareth fear to find his brothers?

28. Who first comes before the King for justice?

29. What contrast is here shown between Uther's idea of justice and Arthur's?

30. What request does the second widow make of the King?

31. Why does Sir Kay urge the King to refuse her request?

32. What decision does the King finally make?

33. What request was made by the messenger of Mark, the Cornish king?

34. How was the request treated by King Arthur?

35. How was rank shown among the knights of King Arthur's court?

36. How were Gareth's brothers ranked by the King?

37. What favor did Gareth ask of the King?

38. What tells of the character of Sir Kay under whom Gareth was to serve?

39. Compare Lancelot and Sir Kay as judges of human nature.

40. Explain "so Gareth, all for glory, underwent the sooty yoke of kitchen vassalage." Select the most vivid descriptive phrases that describe his experiences (lines 486–514).

41. What happenings in Gareth's kitchen service tell of his character?

42. How did Gareth regard the release from his vow?

The Quest of Sir Gareth

43. What secret request did Gareth now make of the King?

44. What incidents tell how Arthur regards Gareth?

45. What instruction did the King give Lancelot?

46. What in the description and incidents given tell of the character of Lynette?

47. What boon or favor does she ask of the King?

48. What four knights did her champion have to overthrow?

49. What boon does Sir Gareth ask?

50. Why does Sir Kay groan when Gareth asks the boon?

51. What tells of Lynette's mood when she finds that Gareth instead of Lancelot is to be her champion?

52. Describe briefly Gareth's departure.

53. What is told further of Sir Kay's character here?

54. Explain Lynette's treatment of Gareth (lines 720–734).

THE RESCUE OF THE BARON

55. What kind of knight does Gareth prove in his first contest (lines 739–740)?

56. How does Lynette regard this bravery?

57. What is shown of Gareth in his answer to Lynette?

58. Where does Lynette first show signs of her dependence on Gareth?

59. What degree of knightly skill is shown in Gareth's rescue of the stalwart Baron?

60. How does Lynette (lines 814–823), as compared with the Baron, interpret this deed?

61. What further is shown of her in her treatment of Gareth in the Baron's hall?

62. How does she explain the fact that the King gave her Gareth for a champion?

63. Why does the Baron suggest that Gareth return for Lancelot?

64. What signs of relenting does Lynette show (lines 870–877)?

MORNING-STAR, NOON-SUN, EVENING-STAR

65. What explanation of Gareth's coming does Lynette give Sir Morning-Star?

66. What signs of display are shown in the court of Morning-Star? Select and interpret the most vivid descriptive phrases by which Tennyson pictures to us the scenes centering in the silk pavilion of Sir Morning-Star (lines 883–916).

67. What effect does Lynette's taunting have upon Gareth?

68. What effect does Morning-Star's taunting have?

69. On what conditions does Gareth spare the life of the overthrown Morning-Star?

70. How does the fact that the "kitchen knave" shows knightly qualities affect Lynette?

71. How does Lynette answer the challenge of Noon-Sun?

72. How did Lynette interpret the second victory?

73. What does Lynette's song indicate as to her mood and her present feeling toward Gareth?

74. How do you account for Lynette's confidence in Gareth's ability to overthrow the Star of Even (lines 1074–1078)?

75. What spurred Gareth on to his third victory (lines 1107–1112)? What vivid descriptive phrases bring the combat vividly before us (lines 1082–1127)?

76. Why does Lynette now command Gareth to ride at her side?

77. What tells of Lynette's changed attitude toward Sir Gareth?

78. How does Gareth excuse her discourtesies?

79. Explain where the four defeated knights got their "allegory."

Accidental Contest and Final Triumph

80. What happened in the accidental contest between Lancelot and Gareth?

81. Why does Lynette now express her hatred for Gareth (lines 1222–1225)?

82. What is shown of Sir Gareth in the words of Lancelot?

83. What request does Lynette now make of Lancelot?

84. How is Lancelot's greatness shown in his answer?

85. How is Gareth's valor shown in his last encounter? By what fitting descriptive phrases does Tennyson picture the encounter at the Castle Perilous (lines 1323–1375)?

86. Why had they disguised a mere blooming boy as Death?

87. Trace the steps by which Lynette came to have faith in Gareth.

88. Write a brief summary of the story.

89. Select three passages which best show the character of Gareth.

90. What are here shown to be the ideals of King Arthur's Round Table?

91. Make a list of the most telling and vivid descriptive phrases Tennyson employs to picture to us the moving pictures of this Idyll.

LANCELOT AND ELAINE

1. Where does this story come in the series of stories comprising the Idylls?

2. In what well-chosen words and phrases is Elaine first described to us?

3. What is shown of her in *guarded* and *sacred*, used in relation to the shield of Lancelot?

4. Why does she place the shield "where morning's earliest ray might strike it"?

5. Why make a silk case for the shield?

6. What is shown by her embroidering the shield's devices upon the case?

7. What is shown by her barring the door and making for herself pretty stories before the naked shield?

8. What sort of maiden is Elaine as shown by this opening paragraph?

9. How did Elaine happen to have the shield?

10. What of Arthur's character is shown by proclaiming the jousts with the diamonds as prizes?

The Prowess of Lancelot

11. How are Lancelot's skill and prowess measured to us?

12. What does he propose to do with the diamonds?

13. What mood is shown by the King's reply, "Yea, Lord, ye know it"?

14. What caused Lancelot to interpret the King's look as he did?

15. What now caused Lancelot to deceive the King?

16. What is shown in "the King glanced first at him, then at her"?

17. Why does the Queen now scold Sir Lancelot?

18. What is the meaning of "Lancelot vexed at having lied in vain"?

19. What is shown of Lancelot in his speech to the Queen (lines 103–119)?

20. What is shown of Guinevere in her talk of the King?

21. Explain "he is all fault who has no fault at all."

22. By what suggestion did the Queen induce Lancelot to go to the jousts?

Lancelot at Camelot

23. How did Lancelot chance to come to the castle of Astolat?

24. What is shown of Lancelot in that the Lord of Astolat at once thinks he is chief of Arthur's knights?

25. Why does Lancelot there ask for a blank shield?

26. Compare Sir Torre and Sir Lavaine.

27. What is the meaning of Lancelot's courtly speech (lines 236–240)?

28. Explain "won by the mellow voice before she look'd."

29. How did Lancelot appear to Elaine?

30. Explain the meaning of lines 253–255.

31. Explain the meaning of "and loved him, with that love which was her doom."

32. How did the Lord of Astolat entertain his guest?

33. What traits of character are shown in Lancelot in the stories he relates?

34. What was the effect of Lancelot's tales and manner on the fair Elaine?

35. Explain the meaning of lines 335–337.

36. Explain "she stood 'rapt on his face as if it were a god's."

37. What request did she now make of Lancelot? What was his answer?

38. How do you account for her clever suggestion as to his complete disguise?

39. What was the effect on Elaine of Lancelot's words, "I never yet have done so much for any maiden living"?

40. What favor did Lancelot give Elaine in return for hers?

LANCELOT GOES TO THE TOURNAMENT

41. Describe in your own words the hermit's chapel.

42. Why does Lancelot now make himself known to Lavaine? What descriptive phrases picture vividly the "peopled gallery" (lines 426–442)?

43. Give a brief description of the tournament as here pictured. Point out the vivid descriptive phrases that give life to the picture (lines 452–505).

44. What is shown of Lancelot by his waiting to see which was the weaker side?

45. What qualities in this unknown knight caused Arthur to think of Lancelot?

46. What figure is used by Tennyson to show how the knights bore down upon Lancelot?

47. What do the following expressions tell us of Lancelot's physical condition: "sweating with agony," "Diamond me no diamonds!" "Prize me no prizes," "down he slid," and "a marvelous great shriek and ghastly groan."

48. What hints throughout the contest tell of Lancelot's character?

49. Where did the wounded Lancelot seek refuge? Give reasons for your answer.

50. How did the King regard the unknown knight? Explain fully.

The Quest of Gawain

51. What is Gawain's mood when sent to deliver the diamond to the unknown hero? What does this tell of Gawain?

52. Why was the King at the banquet "dark in mood"?

53. How great was the King's surprise when told that Lancelot had not staid at court?

54. How tactful is the Queen in explaining Lancelot's change of plan?

55. What causes the distress of the Queen, the news of Lancelot's wound or the fact that he wore a maiden's favor?

56. Select from lines 602–610 the words which best tell Guinevere's mood. Point out the vivid descriptive phrases in the passage.

57. What contrast is shown in the way in which Elaine receives the news of Lancelot's injury?

58. What of Gawain's character is shown in his attempt to win Elaine? Explain fully.

59. What is shown in Elaine's reply to Gawain's question concerning her love for Lancelot?

60. How did Gawain find that the unknown knight was Lancelot?

61. What is shown of Gawain by his leaving his quest to Elaine?

62. How did the King receive his report?

63. What new gossip swept the court? What words are used to tell the nature of the gossip?

64. What was the effect of all this on the Queen (lines 734–739)?

65. What was the relation between Elaine and her father as shown in lines 740–744?

Elaine Tends Her Champion

66. What motives prompted Elaine to want to serve Lancelot?

67. Explain "this fruit is hung too high for any mouth to gape for save a queen's."

68. Explain "being so very wilful you must go."

69. How was Elaine conducted to Lancelot?

70. What does Elaine first see when she enters the cave? Why is she so greatly pleased?

71. Point out the phrases which make the description of Lancelot so vivid.

72. How does Lancelot receive her story and the diamond?

73. Explain her meaning in, "for near you, fair lord, I am at rest."

74. What tells whether or not Lancelot reads Elaine's secret?

75. What measures to us Elaine's love for Lancelot?

76. What hints tell of Elaine's tenderness and care?

77. What effect does her tenderness and care have upon Lancelot?

78. Explain fully the meaning of lines 870–872.

79. Why did the image of one face make "a treacherous quiet in his heart"?

80. What were the holy vows and pure resolves made by Lancelot?

81. What is foreshadowed in Elaine's oft repeating, "him or death"?

The Return to Astolat

82. On their return to Astolat, what request did Lancelot make of Elaine?

83. What is the meaning of Elaine's "I have gone mad. I love you: let me die"?

84. What objection does Lancelot offer to Elaine's request?

85. What tribute does he pay Elaine?

86. Explain her "of all this will I nothing."

87. What counsel does the father give to Lancelot?

88. What discourtesy does Lancelot show Elaine?

89. How could she now wait so calm in the tower again?

90. In what way does Elaine's song interpret her to us?

91. What does Elaine's dream tell of her wish to be taken to court after death?

Elaine's Strange Request

92. How did the father take her request? Sir Torre?

93. What answer did she make to her father's attempt to change her will?

94. What was her final request?

95. Why does Elaine write the letter?

96. Why does she want to be decked like the Queen?

97. Why does she ask to have the barge guided by the dumb old servitor?

98. Why should she carry a lily in her hand with the silken case hung above her? Point out the descriptive phrases which picture vividly the barge and its occupants (lines 1130–1154).

Lancelot and Guinevere

99. How did Guinevere seem to receive Lancelot's request?

100. How in reality did she receive it? Explain, "saw with a sidelong eye the shadow of some piece of pointed lace, in the Queen's shadow, vibrate on the walls."

101. Why does Lancelot speak of the "rumors flying through the court"?

102. Why did the Queen pluck leaf after leaf from the vine?

103. How did she receive the priceless gems?

104. How had Lancelot lost his worth to her?

105. Why does Guinevere suggest that Lancelot add the diamonds to Elaine's pearls?

106. Why, then, does she seize them and cast them into the stream?

The Strange Funeral Cortege

107. What sight meets Lancelot's eyes at this time?

108. Describe briefly the scene that took place in the King's palace.

109. What was the substance of the letter the King found in Elaine's hand?

110. What is told of Lancelot in his speech to the Knights and Ladies?

111. To what extent is Lancelot here telling the truth?

112. How does the Queen receive his speech?

113. What prompts the Queen to suggest that Lancelot might, at least, have saved Elaine from death?

114. What is the effect of Lancelot's frank further explanation?

115. Why does Arthur order that Elaine be buried like a queen?

116. What is shown of Guinevere in, "Forgive me; mine was jealousy in love"?

117. Explain fully the meaning of his answer (line 1342).

Lancelot and King Arthur

118. What words of sympathy did the King now speak to Lancelot?

119. What is the difference between the Queen's sympathy for Lancelot and that of the King?

120. Explain the meaning of Lancelot's answer (lines 1363–1368).

121. Why does Lancelot answer nothing to the King's reference to his being yet unbound?

122. What is shown of Lancelot that he went apart by himself?

123. How in his own mind does he contrast Elaine's love with that of the Queen?

124. What tells us of the depths of Lancelot's anguish?

125. What tells us whether the spiritual or the sensual triumphed in Lancelot?

126. Write a brief characterization of Elaine. Contrast the loves and characters of Elaine and the Queen. What are the best of the vivid phrases by which Tennyson has pictured to us the widely different characters?

127. Write a short analysis of the character of Lancelot as it is here revealed.

128. Summarize in your own words the story of Elaine. What is the best thought you get from it?

129. What characteristics of Tennyson's style do you find in this poem? Cite words, phrases, or passages to illustrate each point in your answer.

The Holy Grail

1. Who was Sir Percivale as shown in the opening passage?

2. Characterize Ambrosius as shown in lines 8–17.

3. Who was the questioner in this tale? The narrator?

4. How could the simple-minded Ambrosius recognize in Percivale a knight from King Arthur's court?

5. What did Percivale say drove him from the Round Table?

6. What did he feel was wasted in the jousts?

7. What tells of the monk's hazy notion of the Holy Grail?

8. What was the Holy Grail and how did it come to Britain?

9. Why was there now necessity to search for it?

10. What had the monk learned from his books concerning Joseph?

A Nun Discovers the Grail

11. What is told us of Percivale's sister in lines 68–82?

12. Explain "With knees of adoration wore the stone."

13. How did she first learn of the Holy Grail?

14. Why did the Confessor think the Grail would come again?

15. What did the maiden decide to do to hasten the return of the Grail?

16. Tell briefly the story the holy nun told her brother Percivale.

17. What commission did she now give her brother and why?

18. What effect did this have on Percivale?

Sir Galahad Catches the Nun's Vision

19. What here tells us of the character of Sir Galahad?

20. What effect did the nun's vision have upon him?

21. Explain the meaning of lines 141-2.

22. What token did the nun now give Galahad for he Quest?

23. What prophecy did she utter for him?

24. Explain fully the meaning of lines 163-5.

25. What was "The Siege perilous"? Explain fully.

26. What fate did Merlin meet in his own chair?

27. Why did Sir Galahad desire to lose himself?

28. What happened after he sat in Merlin's chair?

29. Why was the Holy Grail covered with a luminous cloud?

30. What effect did this wonderful appearance have on the knights?

31. What vow did the leaders now take?

32. Why did Gawain swear louder than the rest?

33. Meanwhile, what had happened to King Arthur?

34. Describe briefly King Arthur's mighty hall.

35. Cite passages showing its richest and mos[t] beautiful features.

KING ARTHUR'S DARK FOREBODINGS

36. What did the king learn on his return?

37. Why did Arthur's face darken when he learne[d] of what had happened?

38. Explain the meaning of the question in line[s] 286-7.

39. What was Galahad's answer to the king?

40. What do this and the king's reply tell u[s] further of Galahad?

41. What in brief is the king's argument against th[e] knights' going in quest of the Holy Grail?

42. What dark prediction did he make?

43. Why did the king request the knights once mor[e] to meet in a tourney before departing?

44. How did Galahad and Percivale acquit them[-]selves at the tournament?

KNIGHTS SET OUT ON HOLY QUEST

45. Describe briefly the picture given us as th[e] knights set out from Camelot.

46. What mixed feelings were now in the heart o[f] Percivale?

47. Tell briefly of his first experience on the Quest[.]

48. If we conceive this Quest as a growth in spiritua[l] power, what does his first experience signify?

49. What was his second experience? What does i[t] signify?

50. Explain briefly his experience with the "Lord of all the world." Tell what you think it means.

51. What was his next experience and its meaning in lines 421–39?

52. What quality did the holy hermit say was lacking in Percivale?

53. How important was this quality for the success of the Quest?

54. What had Galahad done that Percivale had not?

55. What did Galahad see in the holy chapel that Percivale did not?

56. What here shows the extent to which Galahad had caught the holy nun's vision?

Percivale Catches Holy Vision

57. Tell briefly the experiences of Galahad and Percivale as together they pursue the Quest.

58. What vision came to Percivale in these experiences?

59. What further is here told us of the monk, Ambrosius (lines 540–63)?

60. What confession did Percivale make?

61. What now caused the Quest to fade from his heart?

62. Why did he arise at night and fly from the castle of the princess?

63. Why did he care nothing for her when he was with Galahad?

Reports of Lancelot and Sir Bors

64. What account does Percivale give of Sir Bors' quest?

65. Explain Lancelot's statement, "there is a lion in the way."

66. What do lines 650–654 tell us further concerning Sir Bors?

67. What experiences came to him among the pagans?

68. What vision came to him in the great stone prison?

69. How did he escape to tell the tale?

70. In what condition did the returned knights find Arthur's capital city?

71. What situation did the returned knights find in King Arthur's hall?

72. What report did Gawain give of his quest? What does this tell us of him?

73. Tell briefly Lancelot's story of his quest.

74. What characteristics of Lancelot are shown us in the story? Cite passages to prove your answer.

75. Why do you suppose the Grail was "veil'd and cover'd" in the vision of Lancelot?

76. Explain the meaning of the remark with which Sir Gawain broke the long silence.

77. Explain the meaning of the king's rebuke.

78. How many persons in all had seen the Holy Grail? Just how had each seen it?

79. How, according to King Arthur, does the real work of a king differ from that of knights?

80. Tell briefly the story of the *Holy Grail*.

THE PASSING OF ARTHUR

1. What place does this story take in the Idylls?

2. How does Tennyson introduce the story of The Passing of Arthur?

3. How is the King here introduced? Why was Sir Bedivere introduced?

4. How had Arthur's Kingdom "reeled back into the beast"?

5. How was Arthur's death foreshadowed?

6. Who seeks Arthur's throne?

7. Explain "for the ghost is as the man."

8. What does Arthur now most regret?

THE LAST GREAT BATTLE

9. What tells of the severity of this last great conflict? Describe briefly the battle, pointing out the descriptive phrases that bring the picture vividly before us (lines 79–135).

10. What adds to the weirdness of Tennyson's description?

11. To whom does Sir Bedivere point as the arch traitor to the King?

12. Explain fully, "My house hath been my doom."

13. What was Arthur's "last act of knighthood"?

14. How does Sir Bedivere show his full measure of loyalty to the King?

15. Explain, "I perish by this people which I made."

SIR BEDIVERE'S MISSION

16. What command does Arthur now give Sir Bedivere?

17. Whence had Arthur secured his faithful sword Excalibur?

18. What promise did Sir Bedivere make the King?

19. What was the effect on Sir Bedivere of his gazing upon the jeweled sword? Point out the vivid descriptive phrases which picture the beauty and richness of the sword (lines 220–226).

20. Explain, "dividing the swift mind in act to throw."

21. Why did he then conceal the sword among "the many-knotted waterflags"?

22. Why did he go back *slow* to the wounded King?

23. Why did not Sir Bedivere answer directly the King's question?

24. How could the King reply so surely, "Thou hast betrayed thy nature and thy name, not rendering true answer"?

25. What second request did the King make of Sir Bedivere?

26. Why did Sir Bedivere count the dewy pebbles?

Sir Bedivere's Inner Conflict

27. What conflicting thoughts were awakened at sight of the wonderful sword-hilt?

28. What arguments had he for the act? What against it?

29. What conclusion did he reach?

30. Why did he again give the King an evasive answer?

31. How did the repetition of the act of disobedience affect the King?

32. What is the effect of having "the latest-left" of the knights wavering in obedience?

33. What penalty does the King attach to further disobedience?

34. What effect had this speech of the King on Sir Bedivere? Why did he now *run*, *leap*, and *plunge* to do his King's bidding? Point out the vivid descriptive phrases here (lines 301–315).

35. Describe the scene at the mysterious disappearance of the sword.

36. How could the King know, without verbal report, that his command was obeyed?

37. What is now shown of Sir Bedivere in his frank report?

38. Explain, "I closed mine eyelids, lest the gems should blind my purpose."

THE PASSING OF THE KING

39. Why does the King now desire to be taken to the margin of the lake?

40. Explain, "would have spoken, but found not words."

41. Describe briefly the scene here pictured. What phrases make the picture clear (lines 361–371)?

42. What apparition met them on the level lake shore?

43. Who were the "Three Queens with crowns of gold"?

44. What now was Arthur's request?

45. Why was his head placed in the lap of her "that rose tallest—and fairest"? What is the meaning of it all?

46. Describe briefly the appearance of the King at

this time. What vivid words and phrases bring out th picture clearly (lines 373–389)?

47. What is the meaning of Sir Bedivere's lament

48. In what sense was the Round Table "an imag of the mighty world"?

49. Explain fully Arthur's meaning in

> "The old order changeth, yielding place to new,
> And God fulfills himself in many ways,
> Lest one good custom should corrupt the world."

50. What last request does the King make of Si Bedivere?

51. What is the effect of this mysterious passing o the King? How does it harmonize with his mysteriou origin?

52. Explain "From the great deep to the great dee he goes."

53. What do the words of Sir Bedivere reveal as t the current belief in Arthur's second coming?

SUMMARY OF THE IDYLLS

1. Write an interesting sketch of the complete stor; interpreted by the Idylls. If possible, read the com plete poem.

2. Sketch briefly your own interpretation of th larger meaning of the story of King Arthur as reveale in the Idylls.

3. To what extent does the poem reveal the need o coöperation as the foundation for real achievement?

4. Which triumph seems greater in the Idylls, tha of the forces of evil or that of the forces of good?

5. Collect from the poem the choicest short quotations which seem worthy of remembering and the most vivid descriptive phrases. Use these to illustrate a discussion of "The Chief Characteristics of Tennyson's Style."

6. From outside reading, bring in an estimate of the Idylls as given by any two important critics.

7. What in the study of the Idylls has given you the greatest satisfaction and profit?

8. What now seem to be the best reasons for a study of the Idylls? What is the greatest good to be had from the study and appreciation of such a poem?

4. Collect from the poet the hints, short quotations, such seem worthy of its recognition, and the most vivid descriptive phrases. Use these to illustrate a discussion of

5. The Chief Characteristics of Tennyson's style.

6. From outside reading, bring in an estimate of the Idylls as given by any two important critics.

7. What in the study of the Idylls has given you the greatest satisfaction and profit?

8. What has seem to be the best reasons for a study of the Idylls? What is the greatest good to be had from the study and appreciation of such a poem?